FAITHFUL
FAMILIES

raising
your kids
to
love the Lord

DAVE STONE

THOMAS NELSON
Since 1798

NASHVILLE   DALLAS   MEXICO CITY   RIO DE JANEIRO

Raising Your Kids to Love the Lord

© 2012 by Dave Stone

Published in Nashville, Tennessee, by Thomas Nelson®. Thomas Nelson is a registered trademark of Thomas Nelson, Inc.

Designed by ThinkPen Design

Thomas Nelson, Inc., titles may be purchased in bulk for educational, business, fund-raising, or sales promotional use. For information, please e-mail SpecialMarkets@ThomasNelson.com.

ISBN-13: 978-1-4003-2254-1

Printed in China

12 13 14 15 16 [RRD] 5 4 3 2 1

www.thomasnelson.com

Dedication

To Beth

God answered my prayer when you said yes to my proposal twenty-seven years ago. One of your deepest desires was to be a mom. It's obvious why . . . you do it better than anyone I know. Your fingerprints are evident on each page of this book.

Thanks for loving the Lord and me. Can't imagine doing life without you beside me.

Your very grateful husband,

Dave

This book is also dedicated to Life in Abundance International (www.liaint.org).

Your outreach ministry in Kenya has left an imprint on our family that will not fade. You are transforming families in some of the poorest regions of the world. Your prayer life inspires us, your example motivates us, and your love for the least of these compels us.

Dave & Beth

Acknowledgments

Savannah, Sadie, and Sam: You all bring so much joy and fulfillment to my life. This book couldn't have been written unless you each were a godly kid. (Try to stay out of prison at least until this book has been released.)

Patrick: You are an awesome son-in-law. Thanks for your help on the title.

Mom and Dad: Thanks for doing and being what's in this book and a whole lot more.

Lisa Stilwell & Laura Minchew: You have been great to work with and represent Thomas Nelson Publishing and Christ quite well.

Penny Stokes: What can I say, you be very grate writing coach. I tell people you work marigolds with my writing. (You rock, Penny. Thanks for your patience and help!)

Jack Countryman: Thanks for believing in me five years ago.

Thanks to the Southeast Elders for allowing me to write and to Kyle Idleman, Debbie Carper, Laura Williams, Dave Kennedy, along with Jimmy and Macie Allen, for your encouragement. Ben Cross, you're a bloodhound when it comes to finding sources. Thanks!

Thanks to my team of encouragers and readers: the Rusaws, the Harlows, Laurie Allen, Sara Burke, Carl and Lindsay Kuhl, Tish Cordrey, Lance and Kisa Hoeltke, Mary Leslie, Mandy Laurin, Rebecca St. James, and Brenda Harrell. Your insights greatly improved this book.

Table of Contents

1. Top-Button Truths 9

2. Who You Are When No One's Watching 17

3. The Most Powerful Word 31

4. The One Essential Book 47

5. The Key 63

6. A Mother's Heart 79

7. A Father's Gifts 95

8. Sharing the Load 111

9. The Spittin' Image 121

10. The Last Word 133

Notes 142

1

Top-Button Truths

The hallway was packed, but Heather seemed oblivious to the crowds jostling around us. She was new to the church, visiting at the invitation of a friend. We chitchatted for a moment, but the small talk changed dramatically when I asked what she hoped to gain by worshipping with us at Southeast.

Tears filled her eyes, and she said, "Dave, I just want my kids to grow up and love the Lord."

Heather is not alone. Plenty of people want faith for their family.

I do. You do, too, or you wouldn't have picked up this book.

Parents look in a lot of different directions to ensure that the spiritual baton is passed on to their children. Some, like Heather, rely on the church or a Christian school. Others will turn to close relatives, camp, or a parenting book.

I commend those choices; they can all be helpful. But there's a better place to begin.

If you want your kids to grow up to love the Lord, it all starts with . . .

You.

Top-Button Truths

Have you ever gotten to work, or church, or your kid's school play only to look down and realize that your shirt or blouse is buttoned the wrong way?

It's a minor embarrassment, but it's also a metaphor for spiritual truth. If you start at the top and work your way down, the rest of the process comes quite naturally. But if you button the top one wrong, things will be skewed from the start. You can keep on buttoning, but eventually you'll have to start over. It pays to start right from the beginning.

For some, this book is a chance to start over from the top. For others, it's positive reinforcement to stay the course.

In this book you'll find practical suggestions and creative ideas that will be helpful to you regardless of your family dynamics. You'll have a chance to get refocused on those "top-button" truths, the principles that make all the difference in your own spiritual life and in the lives of your children. You'll learn that when your heart truly beats for the Lord, when godly living is your priority, it becomes more natural for your children to embrace faith. Real faith.

I know you're thinking it, so go ahead and ask: "Who is this guy anyway? What makes him such an expert? What gives him any wisdom for my family?"

Well, let me just say right up front that I am *not* a child psychologist. I do *not* have a counseling degree.

I am a parent and a Christian. I love the Lord.

And I've survived.

Does it feel that way sometimes, that all you can do as a parent is survive? I've felt that, too. But I've also experienced those awesome moments of watching our children come to believe and trust in God. I've seen a little faith become a fire; I've seen them mature and settle into their own personal faith. I've watched them grow up to love the Lord.

By the grace of God, my wife, Beth, and I have raised two well-adjusted daughters who love the Lord and a teenage son who shows every sign of following that path. All three of our kids are looked up to by Christians and non-Christians alike.

I say that not with arrogance, but with deep gratitude to the Lord . . . and to Beth.

For years we've had home Bible studies with couples in their twenties and thirties. They all ask the same questions:

- Why do your kids enjoy talking about spiritual things?

- How do you get Sam to look people in the eyes and speak to them?
- How did Savannah keep her faith during college?

And our answer is always the same: we raised our kids to love the Lord, to value others, and to use their gifts for Him.

So when Heather said to me, "I just want my children to love the Lord," something stirred in my soul. Because that's my daily prayer for my own family. And it's also my passion for other families as well, to help parents pass on to their children a fervent and authentic love for God and the heartfelt desire for a genuine relationship with Christ.

Pretenders & Perfectionists

For over two decades I've been privileged to preach at a great church, where over twenty thousand people come to worship God each weekend. So I minister in a setting where I'm exposed to all kinds of families. Some are genuine in their desire to have a family who loves the Lord, but as in most churches, many are *pretenders*. They play the part in a sanctuary on Sunday morning. Once Monday rolls around, however, you'd be hard-pressed to see any difference between them and anybody else on the block.

Other parents are *perfectionists*. They train their children to toe the line and do everything just right for

You'll learn that when your heart truly beats for the Lord, when godly living is your priority, it becomes more natural for your children to embrace faith.

onlookers. They want their kids to perform on cue, like the cocker spaniel who wins Best in Show at the Westminster Kennel Club. But they've never taken the time to address the heart issues or concern themselves with what's on the inside.

Now, Beth and I love our children. They make us proud, and occasionally they disappoint us—just as we do them. Along the way we've made plenty of mistakes. And in the process we've learned some things we can pass on to other struggling parents.

Nobody does it right all of the time.

I remember once watching my three-year-old crawl across the kitchen counter growling like a lion. I asked her, "Does Mommy let you do this?"

She replied, "No—but you do!"

My prayer is that you will learn from both our blunders and our triumphs.

Assembly-Line Spirituality

Some of you will read this book in hopes of discovering an easy gimmick or quick fix for your parenting. Others are looking for a step-by-step guide to ensure fully devoted followers.

If you fall into any of those categories, then I sure hope you kept your receipt! Because there's no such thing as assembly-line spirituality—check off five boxes and *presto*! You've got a Christian child.

People point to Proverbs 22:6, "Start children off on the way they should go, and even when they are old they will not turn from it" (NIV 2011). But that passage is meant to be understood as a general principle, not an iron-clad promise.

Let's face it. Only perfect parents raise perfect children. (Last time I checked, there were no perfect children and no perfect parents either!) There is no foolproof plan. And there's this little detail called *free will*, which will determine the spiritual commitment level of your children when they are grown.

On the other hand, Christian homes don't just happen; neither do kids who love the Lord. There's a lot we can do to help determine the outcome of our children's spiritual lives. We can become intentional in our efforts. We can pave the way for them. We can model true faith and continually pray that God will transform their hearts.

And we can focus on top-button truths.

Whether you have teens or toddlers, whether you're getting ready for graduation or just beginning potty training, you can influence your kids for Christ. The earlier you begin the process, the better—but it's never too late.

The best time to plant an oak tree was twenty-five years ago.

The second best time is today.

If you want your kids to grow up to love the Lord, then join me on this journey. Together let's strive to be the family that God wants us to be. Not a *pretend* family. Not a *perfect* family. But a family whose kids grow up to love the Lord.

2

Who You Are When No One's Watching

T wenty-two-year-old Katie stood in the center of the room with her parents, sister, and closest friends circled around her. This was the moment of truth: her intervention. Her hands trembled and her voice shook as she admitted the gruesome realities of her addiction to drugs and alcohol. Everyone listened intently, and then they began to respond. With candor and honesty they spoke of the pain Katie's addiction had brought to their lives and promised to stick with her during her rehab and recovery. It was a moment of intense anguish and profound healing.

Until it came to her mother.

"Katie," her mom said, "I'm an addict, too. I'm addicted to the Father, Son, and Holy Spirit."

For a moment or two everyone was silent. No one could believe what they'd just heard. Then her daughter looked back at her and said, "Your religion is a joke, and you are a hypocrite."

The remainder of the therapy session revealed the truth about Katie's family: Her parents had taken her to church, but their Christianity was just a big act. They didn't live it. It made no difference at all in their lives or in the way they related as a family.

At fourteen, Katie had had enough. She told her parents, "I don't want to pretend anymore." That night she ran away from home, began experimenting with drugs, and spent years in and out of rehab centers.

A friend of mine witnessed Katie's intervention first-hand. "It gave me chills," he said. "I don't ever want my kids to point their finger at me and say, 'Your faith is a joke and you are a hypocrite.'"

Neither do I.

Show and Substance

Jesus saw a lot of hypocrisy up close and personal. The Pharisees of His day were a lot like Katie's parents. They acted spiritual and claimed a close relationship with God, but it was all a facade. They weren't what they appeared to be. They said the right thing but didn't practice what they preached. And Jesus didn't let them off easy.

He called them "whitewashed tombs . . . full of dead men's bones" (Matthew 23:27).

We have plenty of whitewashed tombs in our generation as well—families who appear to be holy but on closer inspection turn out to be hollow. They're like a chocolate Easter bunny—you think it's solid and filling, but when you break into it, you find nothing but a fragile and empty shell. It's all show and no substance.

When there's nothing inside, when our Christianity is simply a religious pretense, we have no right to expect our children to respect our faith or follow us in it. If we want to grow a family that loves and honors the Lord, that process begins with our authenticity; with the kind of faith that makes a difference in the way we live and love every single day.

That's God's call and challenge to us.

That's the example Jesus set for us.

Warning to Parents

I probably should put a label on this section that reads: *Warning: This chapter may hit too close to home.*
Literally.

But I promise I'm not gunning for you, and I haven't talked to your spouse or your neighbors. If you feel like I've been eavesdropping or spying on your family, know this:

All parents struggle with the same issues. All of us face the same problems and challenges.

Comedian Jim Gaffigan says, "Sometimes I feel unqualified to be a parent. I call those times being awake."[1]

Can you relate? I can.

Nurturing a godly family doesn't happen overnight, and it's not something you can learn from a few bullet points and a how-to article. It demands time and commitment and openness. There are no easy answers—and most of the time there aren't even any easy questions.

The real issue is separating the hollow from the holy, separating pretense from the rigorous investment of time, passion, and prayer to spiritually lead our children. The real issue is living out the call of Christ in our lives as parents.

Jesus reduced the expectation down to this: "But seek first his kingdom and his righteousness, and all these things will be given to you as well" (Matthew 6:33).

So how do we do it? What makes the difference between a family life rich with spiritual substance and a family life based on pretense and image?

It's a simple principle, but an uncomfortable one if we take it to heart: *our children will be more apt to love the Lord if we do.*

Children want
something
that is real;
they want
to follow
someone who
is genuine.

Consistent Living

When parents are fleshing out their faith and living out their days with joy and honesty, their children will be attracted to it. Children want something that is real; they want to follow someone who is genuine. Your example—in victories and challenges, in successes and sins, in forgiveness and accountability—can lead them toward an authentic relationship with the Lord.

But your faith must be both a noun and a verb. It can't be all talk. It's who you are and how you conduct yourself, consistently, daily. It's how your actions grow out of your identity in Christ.

It's the way you act when you are miles away from your family on a business trip. It's how you respond when you are the object of advances from a coworker. It's what you say when a neighbor gossips or a boss pressures you to fudge on the budget.

Character is who you are when no one's watching.

But count on it, your kids *will* watch. They'll pick up on a wandering eye or little white lies. They'll sense deception if you try to paint a rosy picture of your marriage when it's more thorns than flowers. Little eyes watch; little ears listen. They notice everything. They see how you are in public and in private. They have a knack for exposing respectable frauds. When you live under the same roof, it's hard to hide the glaring inconsistencies.

When the phone rings, your spouse answers it, and you silently mouth, "Tell her I'm not here," don't be surprised when your daughter lies to you in order to get herself out of an awkward jam with her grades or her boyfriend.

I've heard it a thousand times. A child takes an unwise detour in high school or college, and the parents come to me saying, "We don't understand. We raised him in the church."

And I want to ask, "But what did you model for him in the home?"

Chris Dewelt, professor of missions at Ozark Christian College in Joplin, Missouri, put it like this:

> I am to be the same person whether I am holding a communion tray in my hand or a remote control. I am to be the same person whether I am in a hotel room five hundred miles from home or in the family room with my kids. I am to be the same person when I am reading my Bible or browsing through a bookstore. I am to be the same person whether I am on break at work or if I am walking through the sanctuary of my church. For what matters is my integrity, my purity, and my faithfulness.[2]

God expects us to be genuine, to do what we say we'll do, and to be who we claim to be. Duplicity is not only exhausting, but it's also damaging to the ones we love. Pretending wreaks havoc in our homes and sends mixed signals to the children we are trying to lead.

Just ask the Katies of the world.

Success and Spirituality

A few years ago I ran into a neighbor coming out of the grocery store. She proceeded to brag on her kids. Both of her children had graduated from college. One had become a doctor, and the other was an accountant. "So," she said proudly, "I guess we were a success as parents!"

As I headed to my car, I had an uneasy feeling in my gut. Don't get me wrong—I want my kids to get a college degree and find gainful employment. But ultimately that's not what will determine whether I've been successful in my parenting. What matters is that my children follow God's leading. It shouldn't make any difference to me if my son becomes a surgeon, drops out of college after a year to serve in a developing nation, or flips burgers down the street. If he is walking with Christ and being responsive to the leading of the Spirit, then I've done my job.

Your faith must be both a noun and a verb. It can't be all talk.

Make no mistake, your sons and daughters will follow your lead and live up to your expectations. If through your parenting you imply that the aim of adulthood is a high-paying job or an expensive house, your children are likely to pursue those goals with more vigor than they pursue their faith.

There's nothing wrong with having a college degree or a nice house, of course. Those things aren't sinful—they're just *things*. And like all things, they must be secondary to loving the Lord. Everything else pales in comparison to a personal relationship with Christ.

And it *is* a personal relationship. Christianity is not about going to church or being outwardly religious. It's about inner faith and commitment. Children don't grow up to love God just because they've been in Sunday school. They grow in spirit because they've had spiritual role models. The goal is for their heart to be in it, for them to care about worship and about faith, not out of duty or obligation, but out of devotion and desire.

Unfortunately, many people today view church as if it were a club membership, a social gathering, a networking opportunity. So instead of loving the Lord, children grow up learning to imitate the faith facade they may have seen around them. When they start their own families, they will continue to perpetuate the cycle of pretending they observed growing up. They'll end up acting one way at church but another way at home, at work, or with the neighbors.

If we want to raise our families to love and serve God, we have to be clear about our priorities. Like Joshua, we have to face up to those around us and say, "If serving the LORD seems undesirable to you, then choose for yourselves this day whom you will serve. . . . But as for me and my household, we will serve the LORD" (Joshua 24:15).

Christian First

A young high school student in Georgia tried out to be a cheerleader. She made the squad, but several weeks into the season, the cheerleading sponsor called a practice on Wednesday evening. The student had made a commitment to attend a Bible study at her church that night, so she told the sponsor and missed the practice.

This galled the sponsor so much that she intentionally changed the practice schedule so that it would regularly conflict with the girl's church commitment. She then said to the student, "If you miss one more practice, you're off the team."

Wednesday night came, and the teen didn't cave to the pressure. She attended her Bible study. The next morning the sponsor of the squad came into her homeroom class and said, "Where were you last night?"

"I thought you knew where I would be," the cheerleader politely said. "I went to church."

"Well, I guess you know what this means—you're off the squad."

"I realize that," the student responded. "I knew it when I chose to keep that commitment to my Bible study. But there's something that you need to know about me. I'm a Christian who just happens to be a cheerleader, not a cheerleader who just happens to be a Christian."

That's our goal in parenting—to raise children who will be Christians first, the same people in private as they are in public, regardless of the consequences. And that type of commitment is usually the result of parents who have both modeled and instilled a faith based on personal integrity.

Evidently the parents of that cheerleader had prepared her early on to take a stand. She had a genuine faith that could face up to an intense challenge, and she didn't give in to pressure or manipulation. Her faith had become her own; by her actions she said, "As for me and my household, we will serve the Lord."

The Task Before Us

So here's my question for you: Are you a parent who just happens to be a Christian, or are you a Christian who just happens to be a parent? A Christian family doesn't magically and instantly appear because we wish it into existence. We have to be serious

That's our goal in parenting—to raise children who will be Christians first, the same people in private as they are in public, regardless of the consequences.

about the task of passing on our faith, about living the way God calls us to live—not just when others are looking, but all day, every day.

If you're like me, you're probably uncomfortably aware of inconsistencies in your parenting and pockets of hypocrisy in your personal life. You can't undo past mistakes; it's impossible to unscramble eggs. But remember Romans 8:1: "There is now no condemnation for those who are in Christ Jesus."

God is more concerned with your *direction* than He is your *perfection*.

He's looking for consistency and integrity. Not pretend religion but genuine faith and trust.

So if you're feeling the strain of your own imperfections, confess to God your inconsistencies, those moments of phoniness that have sent the wrong message to your children. Ask God to help you become authentic and genuinely sold out to Him. The world doesn't need chameleon parents who simply blend in with their surroundings. Your kids need to see you living what you believe.

None of us is perfect—far from it. But we can be genuine and maturing in our relationship with God. We can live our faith with integrity and authenticity. And we can pass that faith on to the next generation.

We can be people who love the Lord and live like it, no matter who is watching.

3

The Most Powerful Word

What's the most powerful word in the English language?

Ask anybody.

Ask the self-help guru who makes a living telling you how to avoid burnout. He'll tell you, "You have to clarify your values and priorities. You have to establish boundaries. You have to learn to say no."

Ask the frazzled mother of a toddler or a teen. She knows: You have to set limits. You have to discipline. You have to be consistent. You have to learn to say no.

Ask any two-year-old. Broccoli? Beans? Bedtime? The answer is always the same: No! no! NO!

They'll all say the same thing for different reasons: *No* is the most powerful word.

Problem is, they're all wrong.

Living on a Prayer

For a parent who loves the Lord and wants to pass that love on to a son or daughter, no isn't the most powerful word.

The most powerful word is *prayer*.

I've heard it a thousand times, and you probably have, too: "I don't know what to do; I don't know how to help. All I can do is pray."

All I can do . . . as if prayer is nothing more than a last resort and a pathetic substitute for action.

The truth is, prayer is one of the most powerful things a parent can do. Praying with your children and for them. Praying in times of crisis and moments of celebration. Praying for no reason at all other than to thank God for His goodness. Letting them hear you pray. Teaching them by example.

Our older daughter, Savannah, was only three, just walking to the car with Beth. It was an ordinary day, sunny, with a nice blue sky and puffy white clouds. The kind of day you might notice but take for granted, depending on how busy you were.

Beth went far beyond just noticing. She pointed toward the sky and said, "Savannah, look. Didn't God make some beautiful clouds?"

Savannah stopped walking, looked up, and gave a thumbs up toward heaven. "Good job, God," she said.

Now, that's prayer. No fluff, no flash. Just a simple, genuine acknowledgment of who God is and what He's capable of doing.

Prayer Changes . . . Me

We've all seen the bumper sticker: *Prayer Changes Things*.

Certainly, we believe that God answers prayers. God intervenes. Miracles happen. Circumstances change.

But the most important thing prayer changes is the person who's doing the praying. And over the years I've learned that when I pray, "coincidences" happen. When I don't pray, they don't happen. Prayer can transform you, your children, and your parenting. It's the most powerful word we can speak. Unfortunately, prayer also is the most untapped resource available to parents.

Oh, we mean well. We just don't think about it until we're in crisis, and then prayer becomes not a life principle but a life raft, a drowning lunge toward any port in a storm. But if we love our families and want our children to grow up to be people who love the Lord, then praying for them ought to be as natural as breathing.

Prayer is one of those top-button truths. It pays to start right from the beginning.

Getting Desperate

Most Americans are addicted to self-sufficiency. We'll wander forty years in the wilderness rather than stop and ask for directions. We'll push ourselves until we drop rather than admit that we can't do it all. Underneath the business suit, the tool belt, the judge's robe, the jeans and sweatshirt, we're all wearing a cape and tights and pretending to be Super-Somebody, savior of the world.

As parents, we coast along, buy into that self-sufficient attitude, and think to ourselves, "I can figure this out on my own." But by the time we wake up, swallow our pride, and ask for divine intervention, our kids are teenagers, and the die has been cast.

Vance Havner was right when he said, "The situation is desperate, but we are not desperate."[3]

Why pray? Because prayer communicates our dependence on God, our comprehension that we are, indeed, desperate for God's presence and help. When we pray, we are enlisting, invoking, *inviting* divine assistance. We're asking God to come in.

But we need to understand what that means. God enters our hearts and our lives and our families by invitation, but He comes as a lifelong resident, not just an occasional visitor who drops in to help now and then.

Prayer communicates our dependence on God, our comprehension that we are, indeed, desperate for God's presence and help.

Prayer can't simply be a fleeting sentence or two thrown heavenward when we're struggling as parents. It's a privilege, and it is to be a priority. It's also a recognition that we are in over our heads.

Maybe you're feeling that sense of desperation now. Maybe things aren't going so well in your family, and you're afraid it's too late to change. Maybe you're wondering if God can reclaim that lost time.

Take it from a young girl who spoke with an angel and discovered herself pregnant with a long-awaited Messiah: "Nothing is impossible with God" (Luke 1:37). This Lord of ours specializes in making something from nothing and bringing beauty from ashes.

Need wisdom for the tough challenges of being a parent? I've got good news for you. "If any of you lacks wisdom, you should ask God, who gives generously to all without finding fault, and it will be given to you" (James 1:5 NIV 2011). Our dependence on God in prayer gives Him an open door to come in and change things.

To change us.

Face it—you're really not Superman. You're not Superwoman. You can't save the world. But as a child of God you have a vast reservoir of power at your disposal.

Tap into that power. Fill up your tank. The task of raising godly kids is too big—and we are too small—for us to start anywhere except on our knees.

The Most Powerful Lesson

In Luke 11, the disciples ask Jesus, "Lord, teach us to pray."

At the National Day of Prayer service in Washington, DC, Senate Chaplain Barry Black raised an interesting question about this passage: "When the disciples chose to ask for some advice from the Lord, they didn't ask Him how to feed a multitude with a boy's lunch. Or how to exorcise demons or walk on water. Instead they said, 'Lord, teach us to pray.'"

Why would that be their question? Evidently they must have noticed a correlation between Christ's power and His prayers.[4] And they were humble enough, at least in this instance, to admit, "I don't know *how to pray*."

Maybe you feel as if you don't know how to pray either. Maybe you've heard a lot of *thees* and *thous* and language that sounds more like Dante than dialogue. Let me assure you, God's not impressed with flowery words, canned clichés, or memorized phrases. He's interested in hearing genuine thoughts that come straight from your heart (see Luke 18:9–14).

Prayer is simply a conversation between you and God. That's it. Period.

And trust me, He really wants to hear from you.

All you have to do is be real. Pray with honesty and authenticity. Model that for your children. Let them see and hear that talking to God can become as natural as talking to one another.

Find a regular time of day and communicate with God what's on your mind and heart about being a parent. Tell Him your joys and fears. Don't hold back from opening up about your doubts and concerns. Think about what you're saying. Respectfully talk to God in the same way that you would converse with a close friend who is older than you.

Pray for your children. Pray with them. Ask them to pray and listen to what they say. Chances are you'll learn what an untainted prayer to God sounds like.

The earlier you start, the sooner they will learn to pray spontaneously and effortlessly. Gradually it will become second nature both to you and your children.

Lead your kids in prayer when you're driving in the car and an ambulance passes you on the highway. Pray for the students as you round the corner by the high school. Pray for children on the playground, the single mother with three rowdy boys, the lonely and forgotten old woman in a wheelchair, the homeless man who pushes his shopping cart on the street. Seize the moment to word simple prayers on behalf of those individuals . . . then back up your prayers by taking your kids to volunteer at the shelter or the nursing home. What's the point of prayer if it doesn't motivate us to action?

Praying is like saying, "I love you." The more you do it, the more natural it becomes.

What to Pray for Your Children

Remember the prayer Jesus taught His disciples? The one that begins, "Our Father in heaven"? Think through it for a minute.

Holy is Your name. Your kingdom come. Your will be done. Forgive us as we forgive others. Lead us not into temptation. Deliver us from evil.

Only one line—one—is a prayer of request: *Give us the bread we need for this day.*

That doesn't sound much like our prayers, does it? We tend to forget about adoration and thanksgiving and repentance as we focus on "gimme, gimme, gimme."

Of course we want the best for our children. Of course we want their needs to be met. It's fine to make requests of God. But we also need to spend time in prayer adoring and thanking God, focusing on character and inner strength and divine guidance for our children.

Pray for Particular Needs

Our daughter Savannah was in the eighth grade when she decided she wanted to transfer to another school. Beth and I didn't think the switch was a good idea, but we believed that if we turned the situation over to God, He would guide us. All of us.

So we bit our tongues and agreed that together we all three would commit it to prayer.

Maybe it seems risky, giving a teenager a vote in such a decision. But the Lord spoke—quietly to Beth and me, but loudly to Savannah, telling her that He wanted to use her in the school where she was already established. She responded to that calling, stayed put, and became a very respected leader—including senior class president.

If that sounds mystical, asking your children to pray for wisdom or some "answer from on high," then think about Samuel. He was just a boy when God called to him in the night, but with Eli's nudging he answered God's call: "Speak, LORD, for your servant is listening." And he went on to become one of Israel's greatest prophets (1 Samuel 3:9).

Maybe your children need to practice self-control or show kindness to a sibling. Perhaps they need courage to make wise and God-honoring choices.

Teach them to pray.

Trust them. Trust God.

Give it a try. You'll be amazed.

Pray That God Will Guard Their Hearts

My wife and I try to pray daily for our children. I do pretty well, but Beth has it down to a fine art. Most days she will pray through a process for each of them.

Praying is like saying, "I love you." The more you do it, the more natural it becomes.

- *Spiritually*—for spiritual growth and love for the Lord to increase
- *Physically*—for health and safety
- *Sexually*—for purity in mind and body
- *Mentally*—for clear minds so they can make wise choices
- *Emotionally*—for protection from emotional harm
- *Relationally*—for their friendships and for their future mates

Everything on this list is important, of course, but praying for our children's relationships is particularly vital if we want them to grow up to love the Lord. Peer pressure is a powerful force in a young person's life. Friends can make or break your child's relationship with God. When our kids were born, we began to pray that God would bring friends into their lives—and ultimately a spouse—who would be partners on their spiritual journey. It's a prayer that can change the course of your child's life.

All this prayer takes time and focus and effort, of course; it is a huge investment. But such an investment will produce eternal rewards in our children's lives.

Pray That They Will Come to Love the Lord

Makes sense, doesn't it? If you want to be a family whose kids love the Lord, then pray that they will come to love the Lord. Pray that they will find and embrace a radical, biblical faith. Pray that they will adopt it for themselves, not just because Mom and Dad do it, but because they've experienced the grace and goodness and presence of God. Pray that they choose it—not just once, but every single day. And pray that such a decision becomes the natural expression of what's inside their hearts.

The Practice of Prayer

The Bible says, "Pray continually" (1 Thessalonians 5:17). That doesn't mean walking around on our knees; it means living in a spirit of prayer, aware of God's presence around and within us. Listening for His voice. Seeing His hand in the major events of life and in the small daily graces.

But it's all too easy to get busy and sidetracked, so it's important to have some regular, intentional times set aside for prayer and to build the practice into your life and the lives of your children.

Think you don't have time? Author John Piper recently tweeted, "One of the great uses of Twitter and Facebook will be to prove at the Last Day that prayerlessness was not from a lack of time."[5]

A truer tweet was never twitted. We make time for whatever is a priority in our lives.

Pray before you start your day. Our family makes it a priority to pray together before the kids leave for school each day. In the early years it was typically just three minutes. More recently it's become a longer prayer time with our son three mornings each week. Regardless of whether it's three minutes or thirty, it communicates, "Your day is important to me and to God."

Try it. Just a brief huddle-up before the day begins. Share your concerns for the day with them and in turn listen to theirs. Ask for prayer about tests, field trips, meetings, or challenges. Pray for what's going on during your day and theirs. Praise God for how He is working. Depending on the ages of your children, you may get some resistance, but if it's not up for discussion, soon they'll accept it and may even look forward to it.

Pray at specific or significant times. Years ago I was approached with a request to pray daily at 11:17 for a young man who had drifted from the Lord.

Why 11:17? Because that's when the boy was born. And in our prayers we joined the boy's father in asking God for a *new* birth.

God answered that prayer with a resounding yes!

Eleven-seventeen. The exact time of day his son was ushered into this world. And because that boy's dad was so creative in his own prayers, every one of us in that group remembered to stop and pray no matter what we were doing.

Pray before going to bed. When the light goes out, in the safety of their own bed, your kids may share prayer requests or concerns they'd never dare say to you (or God) in broad daylight.

When I was growing up, I remember my mom or dad praying with me by my bed almost every night. One phrase stuck in my mind, both the words and the sense of anticipation they conveyed: "Lord, I can't wait to see how you are going to use Dave for Your glory." It was a seed planted in my mind: I could have a great faith instead of a small faith, and I could wonder not *if* God could use me, but *how* He would use me.

It was the most powerful word in my life.

Make Me Dangerous for God

Eight-year-old Aaron had just attended church camp for the very first time. His dad, author and preacher Erwin McManus, thought it would be a good experience, but the boy came home troubled and frightened and wanting to sleep with the lights on in his bedroom. Turned out, the counselors had told the campers *demon* stories.

"Pray for me, Daddy," Aaron pleaded from his bed. "Pray that God will make me safe."

McManus leaned down and said, "I can't do that, son. I can't pray for God to make you safe."

Aaron's eyes welled up with tears. "But, Daddy, I'm scared. Please pray that God will make me safe."

"I'm not going to pray that God will make you safe," McManus repeated. "I am going to pray that God will make you dangerous, so dangerous that when *you* enter a room, all the demons will have to flee!"

"All right, Dad," Aaron said. "Then pray that God makes me *really* dangerous."[6]

Do you want to raise children who love the Lord? Then prayer is essential, for you and for them.

If you believe in the power of prayer, nothing is important enough to get in the way. You'll find the time. You'll make the investment. You'll bring to God your fears and hopes and dreams for your children, and you'll commit your kids into His care.

Give yourself to prayer for and with your children. You'll see firsthand God's mighty work in their lives. And they'll learn a valuable lesson. *They can do nothing apart from the Lord.*

You and your family will become dangerous for God.

And you'll discover that the most powerful word is prayer.

4

The One Essential Book

Here's a hint: it's not this one.

In the Valley of the Shadow

The road was slick with rain and the sky was dark.

It happened in an instant. As the oncoming car maneuvered around the curve, its back end began to fishtail. The tires hydroplaned on the wet pavement, and the vehicle slid into the opposing lane.

The head-on collision came with a sickening crash of shattering glass and crumpling steel. Then everything grew quiet, except for one quivering voice:

"The LORD is my shepherd; I shall not want..."

That voice belonged to my father, whose face had struck the steering wheel. He had twenty-one shards of glass in his eyes. Behind him in the backseat, my mother was bleeding out from a life-threatening skull fracture.

In the distance we heard the howl of sirens approaching through the rain. But above the wail of the ambulances, the words kept coming: "*Yea, though I walk through the valley of the shadow of death, I will fear no evil; for thou art with me.*"

It is one of the most vivid memories of my childhood.

This was no foxhole prayer, no panicked appeal in a time of crisis. It was Dad's default position. Quoting Scripture was natural and normal for him, whether in the valley or on the mountaintop. My father knew that the Bible offered words that help and heal, words that deepen joy and lessen sorrow. He found strength and connection with God in the Scriptures. Even in that moment of shock and pain and bewilderment, even when he thought his wife was dying, he instinctively turned to the Bible the way others turn to terror.

He depended on the Word of God.

So what's your default position? What do you depend on? What's your strategy to ensure that a transfer of faith to your children happens in your home?

Luck?

A self-help book?

Or something far more important?

Dwelling in the House of the Lord

Want your children to love God? Want them to follow in the way of Jesus? Want them to dwell in the house of the Lord forever?

Then while you've got them dwelling in your house, make it a house of the Lord. Make your house a place where the timeless teachings of the Bible come to life and the principles of the Word are the principles you live by. Let the Author of that book be visible in you.

Henry Blackaby, author of the Bible study *Experiencing God*, says, "You don't just want your children to know the Bible story of Daniel; you want to raise up a Daniel. You want your son to know about the life of Samuel, but even more important, you want him to *become* a Samuel who is always listening to the call of his Father. You want your daughter not just to know the story of Esther, but to *become* an Esther."[7]

He's right.

It doesn't matter how much you know about the Bible or even how much you've memorized. What matters is the kind of relationship you have with the One who wrote it.

You spend time on the Internet. You spend time perfecting your golf swing or learning about online investing. You spend time at the gym or in the mall or at the ballpark. Why not spend some time investing in God's Word and passing that investment on to your family?

Teach Scripture

When your children are preschoolers, get in the habit of telling them Bible stories at bedtime. It's an excellent time to teach. In that familiar setting they will absorb what they hear, and you will benefit from the review of the familiar lessons.

If you don't know the Bible very well, let that motivate you to learn it right along with them. Your young children will ponder the power of God as they fall asleep. And as your kids mature, you'll be learning scriptural truths together.

There's a temptation to leave the teaching of the Bible to the Sunday school teachers and youth ministers of your church. *After all*, you may think, *they know a whole lot more about it than I do.*

But go on. Look in the front of your Bible. Does it say, *For professionals only* or *Don't try this at home*? Mine doesn't. Evidently God wants us to read it—especially in the home. We have a responsibility to learn the Scripture and to teach it to our children. In fact, the Bible is pretty explicit about it:

> Love the LORD your God with all your heart and with all your soul and with all your strength. These commandments that I give you today are to be on your hearts. Impress them on your children. Talk about them when you sit at home and when you walk along the road, when you lie down and when you get up. Tie them as symbols on your hands and

If you don't know the Bible very well, let that motivate you to learn it right along with [your children].

bind them on your foreheads. (Deuteronomy 6:5–8)

The church has a limited window of time with your child. Maybe fifty hours a year. But moms and dads get between two and three *thousand* hours of flexible time in the home every year.

That might sound like a lot. But time's a wastin', so start now. Deuteronomy says that we need to impress God's Word on our children all the time, throughout our daily lives, wherever we are.

How do you do that? You look for teaching opportunities.

If your kids are popular with the in crowd, teach them how Jesus welcomed everyone. If they're feeling isolated and left out, remind them how the Lord took time for hurting people. Do they have to change schools and start over in the middle of the year? Help them see themselves in the story of the Exodus, the parting of the waters, the journey to a new Promised Land.

When your kids feel like they're backed against a wall, show them how Joshua prayed until the walls fell down. Teach them the Bible truths that will help them weather storms and walk on water and put their roots down deep into God's Word. If you facilitate the connections between their life stories and the stories of the Bible, they'll come to realize that the Bible was written thousands of years ago, but it's still relevant to what they face every day.

Lindsay is the young mother of a four-year-old. When she disciplines her daughter, Reagan, she will sometimes say, "Jesus teaches in the Bible that we should be kind. What you did wasn't a kind thing to do. We are trying to become more like Jesus, so we don't do things like that."

It's a practical, down-to-earth way of applying biblical truth on a daily basis: "Impress [these commands] on your children. Talk about them when you sit at home" (Deuteronomy 6:7). Lindsay is deliberately filling her daughter's heart with God's Word.

Display God's Word

Have you ever gone into a house where the Word of God is strategically placed as part of the decor? Instantly the room is transformed, and the values of those who live there are made known.

Jewish families often place a mezuzah at the entryway of their homes—a small case made of metal or wood, containing a parchment with these very verses from Deuteronomy. It's literal obedience to the command "Write [these words] on the doorframes of your houses and on your gates" (Deuteronomy 6:9).

When I was in middle school, my mom put a plaque with a verse on it right at our bathroom sink. Whenever my brother and I would brush our teeth or wash our hands, we'd see those words, over and over and over again: "A gentle answer turns away wrath, but a harsh word stirs up anger" (Proverbs 15:1). It was Mom's subtle (or not-so-subtle) way of trying to curtail the verbal battles that Jeff and I would regularly have.

Displaying Scripture in your home not only exposes your children to God's Word, but it sets a mood and sends a message to others that there is something distinctive here. Your home is a haven for truth, an environment conducive to a spiritual foundation.

It says to all who enter, "This is a house of the Lord."

Memorize Scripture

I know, I know. Some of you are thinking, "Memorize the Bible? I struggle to keep my kids' names straight!"

But trust me, it's important.

King David wrote these words as a prayer to God in Psalm 119: "I have hidden your word in my heart that I might not sin against you" (v.11).

There's value in memorizing Scripture. It stays with you. It helps you conquer temptation, as Jesus modeled during His own temptation in the wilderness (Matthew 4:1–11). Memorizing Scripture facilitates the transfer of truth from your head to your heart.

And if you don't think your children are able to learn, explain, and retain Bible verses, just try them. When my son, Sam, was five, he memorized and could quote twelve consecutive verses from Matthew 5. Each night when he would go to bed, he would listen to a recording of his

Memorizing Scripture facilitates the transfer of truth from your head to your heart.

family members reading that passage to him. Through repetition, it became second nature to him. And he knew what those verses meant, too. He understood them—sometimes better than I did.

Try posting a brief memory verse in your child's bedroom. Stick it to the refrigerator or write it on the bathroom mirror. Put it where you and your children can see it, every day, several times a day. And let it stay there until everyone has learned it.

Back in the 1940s, when J. Russell Morse was serving as a missionary to Kunming, China, in the province of Yunnan, he was imprisoned by the Chinese communists for preaching the gospel. He was in prison for two-and-a-half years, fifteen of those months in solitary confinement. And he was not allowed to have his Bible with him.

After his release, people asked him, "How do you handle something like that? How do you keep your sanity?"

"The only thing I had to hold on to," Morse said, "were the Scriptures I had memorized." In his mind he'd go through the Bible and quote verses to himself. And out of all of the passages he had committed to memory as a child, the one that sustained him most were words written by another prisoner, a man named Paul:

> Do not be anxious about anything, but in everything, by prayer and petition, with thanksgiving, present your requests to God. And the peace of

God, which transcends all understanding, will guard your hearts and your minds in Christ Jesus. (Philippians 4:6–7)[8]

You may have your doubts that you or your children or grandchildren will ever be imprisoned for the faith, but the truth is, we don't know what will be going on in the world twenty or forty or sixty years from now. J. Russell Morse probably hadn't included incarceration in a communist prison on his bucket list either. But there he was, and God's Word was in the cell with him.

We can't know what the future holds or what our children may experience as committed Christians. But we can know that whatever life brings to them, filling their minds with the Word of God is a gift that will last a lifetime and beyond.

Read Your Bible

Recently I did an informal survey of around one hundred young parents, and one of the questions I asked was "Looking back at your upbringing, what do you wish your parents had done differently to help you build a strong spiritual foundation?"

The top response surprised me: "I wish I had seen my parents reading the Bible."

Now, typically my devotional time isn't done at the house. I go to the office and read God's Word to start my day. But I realized, hearing the responses to that survey, that I need to be more intentional about letting my family see my love for the Scripture. My kids shouldn't just *know* that I'm in God's Word; they need to *see* me reading it, too.

And start early, for your kids' sake. Some parents postpone such an emphasis, rationalizing that there will be plenty of time later to emphasize the reading, study, and memorization of God's Word.

But there's a reason that marketing firms go after the four- to twelve-year-olds.

Christine Lagorio of CBS News reported that: "In 1983, companies spent $100 million marketing to kids. Today, they're spending nearly $17 billion annually. That's more than double what it was in 1992."

And evidently they are succeeding. "Eight- to twelve-year-olds spend $30 billion of their own money each year and influence another $150 billion of their parents' spending."[9]

If marketing companies can have that kind of effect on the spending habits of kids, imagine what impact a constant connection to the Bible might have on their lives. Early in adolescence, children establish habits that will stay with them the rest of their lives. Begin early to expose your children and teens to God's Word. The Lord promises that there will be a return on that investment (1 Peter 1:24–25).

Model Scripture

Want to transfer your faith into your kids' lives? Then live it. Do it. Obey it. We're told, "Do not merely listen to the word, and so deceive yourselves. Do what it says" (James 1:22).

Your example teaches your kids the importance of God's Word in their lives. Remember that passage from Deuteronomy 6—the one we read earlier? Look again at verse 6: "These commandments that I give you today are to be on *your* hearts" (emphasis added).

In other words, the starting point for instilling faith in the hearts of your children is that *your* heart believes that the Lord is God. And that *you* love Him with all of your heart, soul, mind, and strength.

Sooner or later you will drive your son or daughter to a college campus to enroll or to her first apartment. You'll unload boxes of belongings: clothes and a computer, posters and magazines, books and a Bible. Then you'll kiss her good-bye and walk to your car with tears rolling down your cheeks. It's a surreal moment of cutting the umbilical cord—for the second time. The instant you pull away, your child will experience a rush of independence greater than anything she's felt before.

And the whole journey back home you'll be thinking . . .

I hope she got it.

I pray that she knows beyond a shadow of a doubt that the Bible is more important than any textbook she will study in her next four years.

I pray that she'll come home the same way that she left our house, as a Christian who is committed to God and His Word.

You've taught and modeled and mentored. Then it's time to entrust your children to God.

All God's Words Are True

J acob was two years old.

His parents had posted a Bible verse on the refrigerator and worked tirelessly with him to help him memorize it. It said, quite simply, "All your words are true" (Psalm 119:160).

Every time Jacob stretched up on his tiptoes to open the refrigerator door, he would point to where the words were posted and say to God, "All your words are *true*!" And he'd hit the refrigerator as he said the word *true* for a little extra emphasis.

And then one day, in an instant, Jacob somehow got the outside door open and wandered out onto the patio, toward the family's swimming pool. . . .

Two years old. In a heartbeat, he was gone.

I conducted the funeral service—the hardest one I've ever done—and concluded with this observation:

I find it interesting that a two-year-old had a Bible verse memorized. It's also amazing that the only verse

The starting point for instilling faith in the hearts of your children is that *your* heart believes that the Lord is God.

he could quote contained the very words that God knew all of us would need on this difficult day. For when tragedies strike, we're tempted to question God and doubt the Bible. We think, How will we make it through? Where can we find our strength? Does God really care? *And then we remember—all God's words are true.*

As I preached at little Jacob's funeral service, I thought about my own family's car wreck so long ago—how we sat stunned in that crush of steel and glass, waiting for the ambulance to arrive, not knowing if Mom would live to see another day. In the midst of that terrible trauma, I heard my father quoting Scripture. He turned to the Lord and to the verses that were engraved upon his heart. And that simple psalm had a greater impact on me than the car that hit us.

By the grace of God, we all survived that accident. My dad's voice brought me peace, and his passion for Scripture planted a seed in my heart.

Don't wait until it's too late to realize what's at stake. Raise your kids with the end goal in mind. You and your family will face transitions and tests, adversity and challenges—some mundane, some monumental. It may not be a disastrous car wreck or an accidental drowning in the family pool . . . but it will be something.

And when that something happens, when the sirens of life begin to wail, what will your children hear *you* say?

5

The Key

The key.

The very word conjures up excitement and anticipation—images of secret places and unimaginable riches, lush gardens, trunks full of treasure, and houses with hidden passageways.

When it comes to raising godly kids, we're all searching for a key. Some switch we can flip that makes things easy . . . or at least possible.

But sometimes the task feels downright impossible.

Consider Ross Brodfuehrer's words and see if they don't feel just a bit familiar:

We have all seen him. This five-year-old demands a Snickers bar from his dad and won't take no for an answer. He wears his dad down along with half the customers and eventually leaves the store with his mouth full and his hands sticky.

Who hasn't stopped behind a school bus only to receive a special sign from an angel in the back? How do we turn out kids who will encourage the handicapped rather than make fun of them, who graffiti their Bibles with insights rather than bathroom stalls with profanity? Is it possible?[10]

Is it? Is it possible to raise children who will respect and obey?

The short and simple answer is "Yes, it's possible." But the process isn't short, and it's certainly not simple.

Ah, and you thought you were going to get a break this time.

The Challenge

A father was watching television with his fourteen-year-old daughter when a program came on about death, dying, and unexplained mysteries. The man said, "Honey, remember this while you're young—you need to live every day as if it were your last."

"I tried that once," she said, "and you grounded me for a month."

The Bible's pretty clear about the issue of discipline, and unfortunately (or fortunately) it doesn't give us much wiggle room: "Children, obey your parents in the Lord, for this is right" (Ephesians 6:1).

That's rather straightforward. But there's a catch. Getting your children to obey is right, but right doesn't always equal easy. Discipline is one of the most challenging aspects of parenting.

Part of the problem is that we have a tendency to see discipline as something negative rather than constructive. Besides that, most of us feel ill-equipped for such an important task. We feel unqualified to be parents—at least when we're awake.

Unqualified. Yes. Also unprepared, unmotivated, and sometimes even uninterested. Our tendency is to parent the way we saw it modeled. And for some parents, that means not at all.

United Front

No family expert can go ten minutes without using the words *united front*. And that's good—it's a pivotal concept, especially in the area of discipline. Your five-year-old can sniff out weakness like a shark smells blood. Just let Dad show signs of caving in, and the child will sense in a heartbeat where the parental alliance is most fragile. Junior will instantly gravitate to that "weaker" parent and stay close until the stronger parent has acquiesced.

Now, I can just hear you new parents saying, "This Dave Stone is a *mean, mean man*. My precious little baby Sophie will never do that."

Just wait. And in the meantime, ask the veterans who can give you a dozen examples—from last week alone.

God's Discipline

On any level, a united front is essential. But if the united front happens to be a couple committed to reflecting godly values through their parenting . . . well, the front just got higher, and the power got stronger.

Let's begin by looking at the way God disciplines His children. It's a model for how you and I should discipline ours.

First, we need to remember that discipline grows out of love. "My son, do not make light of the Lord's discipline, and do not lose heart when he rebukes you, because the Lord disciplines the one he loves" (Hebrews 12:5–6 NIV 2011).

God wants what's best for His children, and He wants to enable us to reach our maximum potential. He disciplines us because He loves us and wants us to grow in His image and likeness. We discipline our children because we love them as well. It's as simple as that.

Getting your children to obey is right, but right doesn't always equal easy. Discipline is one of the most challenging aspects of parenting.

The Key to Discipline

Okay, you've been waiting for the key. That magical golden key that will open every door and bring spiritual treasures to your feet. The key that will enable you to train your children in the knowledge and love of the Lord. The principle that will motivate instead of infuriate.

So here it is: CONSISTENCY.

That's it?

Yep. That's it.

What's lacking among most parents is consistency in their dealings with their children. Consistency has the ability to turn arguments into discussions and complaints into compliance.

If you've ever been tempted to lessen a punishment . . .

If you spend your days repeating instructions and shouting threats . . .

If you sense at times that your kids are calling the shots . . .

Then read on, and join me in learning about how God consistently disciplines His children. Trust me, He's not gonna mind if you steal a few of His ideas.

The Consistency of God

God is the very essence of consistency. His universe emanates it. The sun rises and sets on the reliability of the Lord.

The Father, Son, and Holy Spirit are in complete unity, consistent in their expression of who God is.

"I the LORD do not change" (Malachi 3:6).

"Jesus Christ is the same yesterday and today and forever" (Hebrews 13:8).

Your discipline shapes your child's view of God. It's another way to model a healthy relationship with the Lord and encourage your children to follow in God's way.

Think about the words *discipline* and *disciple*. The root word is the same, and the end goal is the same: coming alongside to teach, train, and model. That's why God sent Jesus to show us the way, so that we could follow in His steps.

Sounds like what we parents are trying to do with our kids.

Consistent Expectations

Children are innately curious and inquisitive. Very early on a child will start pushing boundaries and testing limits. It's an innate desire to try to test the system, to find out where the lines are drawn and what freedoms they have.

James Dobson explains:

> This testing has much the same function as a policeman who turns doorknobs at places of business after dark. Though he tries to open the doors, he hopes that they are locked and that everything

is secure. Likewise, a child who assaults the loving authority of his parents is greatly reassured when their leadership holds firm and confident.[11]

Communicate your expectations clearly. Kids inherently want and need boundaries. Discipline and structure communicate compassion and concern, regardless of the age of your children. And parents who skip through the discipline stage in an effort to be their child's friend are building the future of their family on a fragile foundation.

Proverbs 29:17 says: "Discipline your son, and he will give you peace; he will bring delight to your soul."

Take charge now.

Consistent Voice

It is easier to have that unified front with your children when both parents are getting their instructions from the same Book.

Teach your children to obey you the first time, just as God expects us to obey the first time when He asks— immediately. If your children do it for their earthly parent, in time it will become an easier transition to obey their heavenly Father the first time.

A number of years ago our family was in the Dominican Republic on a mission trip. If you've ever driven in a developing country, you know how dangerous the traffic can be.

Vehicles whiz by, coming within just a few feet of children playing close to the road.

One night my son, Sam, was playing a game in his own little world where he would zig and zag, back and forth from sidewalk onto the narrow street and back. It wasn't a heavily travelled road, but there was always loud music blaring and it was pitch dark. From about ten feet away I suddenly shouted, "Samuel, don't move!"

Immediately he froze. About a second later a Moped zipped past him, going 30 mph with no lights on. Right where Sam was about to step.

My six-year-old didn't ignore me or argue or blatantly disobey. I said freeze, and he froze. That obedience might have saved his life.

But that moment of obedience wasn't a fluke, and it didn't happen automatically. It was the result of months of training and disciplining Sam in plenty of nonthreatening situations. We had set our expectations high and trained him to respond. And when it counted, Sam passed the test.

Consistency always pays off.

Consistent Consequences

Children shouldn't have to guess if they will be disciplined for an action or behavior. They should know. They should also know that the intent and magnitude of the unacceptable behavior will determine the severity of the punishment.

And don't be fooled. Your little angel is slicker than any personal injury lawyer plastered on a forty-foot billboard. If you let her, she can talk her way to a reduced sentence faster than you can blink. You have to be consistent. Otherwise your irregularity muddies the water and allows black-and-white issues to become gray. When that occurs, it's tough to dole out consequences.

Typically your requests aren't up for debate, but in some settings they may be up for discussion, given the right spirit and the right time. There's a difference between arguing and discussing. Let your kids make their appeal and listen to their rationale. Allow them to make a case for *why*. You might gain new information that changes your mind.

Many parents allow their children to dictate when they go to bed or what they eat or what they watch on television. But making decisions is an earned right, not an entitlement. A three-year-old has no business bargaining with a parent. No good can come from catering to the whims of the child.

Obedience comes from love, fear, or respect for the individual. The home has no peace if the parents have no backbone. Inconsistent parents will pay the price over and over again for years to come.

Train your children. Begin when they're toddlers. Impose consequences for their actions the first time instead of the third, or the fifth, or at the point when you're pulling your hair out. Let them know you take your role as parent seriously. Teach them to obey the first time you ask.

Discipline and structure communicate compassion and concern, regardless of the age of your children.

In other words, when you tell your twelve-year-old daughter it's time for her friends to head on home, she knows she can't complain, whine, or drag her feet to share the news with her girlfriends. She just obeys without an attitude or rolling of the eyes.

"When my five-year-old daughter doesn't listen the first time," one mother told me, "I ask her what Ephesians 6:1 says. She can rattle off the verse and usually does what she is told. But when she says, 'I can't. It's too hard,' we have started teaching her Philippians 4:13: 'I can do all things through Christ who strengthens me' (NKJV)."

Wherever you set the bar is the level to which they will rise. If you allow your children to respond the third time when you scream or after you count to three, then you're sending the wrong message. First-time obedience is merely where you as a parent choose to place the expectation.

Consistent Stability

Let's admit it: it's tough to be consistent. Sometimes one parent may be more lenient than the other. Perhaps there's been a divorce and there's a battle between the two homes. One tends to allow more privileges in hopes of getting the upper hand in the relationship.

Sometimes inconsistency is due to working parents who come home exhausted, and the last thing they want to do is enforce rules and battle their child's will. They lack the time, energy, and resolve. But such an environment becomes a seedbed for inconsistency.

If an unacceptable behavior is allowed one day but disciplined the next, your child will be confused. Confusion leads to testing the waters to see what they can get away with. Varying voices make the task so much more difficult.

The good news is that disciplining and training your children doesn't have to be exhausting or frustrating. It just has to be consistent. If your kids know what to expect when they disobey, you establish a pattern that leads to peace and stability in the home.

When God's Word or God's Spirit or God's delegated authority agent (hint: that's *you* as a parent) says to do something, the immediate response should be obedience. You are preparing your children to do the same when they are prompted by their heavenly Father—to say, as Mary did, "I am the Lord's servant. May it be to me as you have said" (Luke 1:38).

You are teaching them that obedience is God's love language.

Consistent Attitudes

When disciplining, we need to remember that attitudes need to be addressed as well as actions. Actions are visible, so sometimes we simply punish the blatant behaviors that others see. But we need to go deeper than just what is on the surface. If you don't get to the root of the sour spirit, complaining attitude, or passive disobedience, you'll never change the actions. Behavior is an outgrowth of belief: what your kids do reveals what's really going on in their hearts. Invested parents are concerned with getting to the *why* beneath the *what*. So keep training them—inside and outside—in the way they should go (see Proverbs 22:6).

Without discipline, chaos rules, love erodes, and inconsistency prevails.

Consistent Relationship

The closer the bond you have with your children, the easier it becomes for them to accept your discipline. Josh McDowell says, "Rules without a relationship lead to rebellion."[12] Countless times I've repeated that to myself as a reminder to keep the communication lines open and to invest more in the relationship than the expectation.

The truth is, all of us have rebelled. There is a time to discipline, there is a time to repent, and there is a time to forgive. You as the parent are establishing the routine, the rules, and the expectations. Because that's what a good parent does.

Parenthood is modeled on the relationship between God and us: He is the Creator; we are the creation. He has the right to call the shots. So do we as parents.

This all takes awhile to teach, but it sure beats years and years of repeated requests and manipulative attempts by your children to get their way. Consistency in discipline

Consistency in discipline will remove the guesswork from parenting and reduce the drama in your home.

will remove the guesswork from parenting and reduce the drama in your home.

My pastor friend Chip Ingram says, "The parent who balances love and discipline, without compromising either, produces well-adjusted kids who maintain a positive relationship with Mom and Dad."[13]

Is it possible to raise children who will respect you and obey you? Yes—in fact, it's easier than you think. Once you've taken time to establish the expectations, discipline with love, and continue with consistency, you'll find the results quite liberating.

The key is consistency, and it opens the door to freedom.

6

A Mother's Heart

t three-and-a-half years old, Sam was an outgoing and effervescent kid. He had been having fun with his sisters all summer, but now they had gone off to school and left him behind, and his whole personality changed. His demeanor was different; the lack of activity in the house seemed to silence his soul.

My wife, Beth, noticed and determined to take advantage of a teachable moment. "Samuel," she said, "I want you to do something for me. I want you to stand right where you are, and I want you to imagine that this room has a long line of three-year-olds."

Beth's eyes began to scan the invisible lineup. "There's one with dark hair; over here is one with light hair. Big noses, little noses. Blue eyes, brown eyes." She regarded him seriously. "All sorts of different children."

Sam started looking around as if to say, *Where are these kids?*

"Now let's see," Beth went on. "If I could choose any one of these kids to be my son, which one do you think I would choose?" She started looking up and down the imaginary row. Samuel grew very still, stood up as straight as he could, and kept looking right into her eyes.

Finally she knelt down in front of him. "I know. I choose the one with the blond hair, and the brown eyes, and the big, big smile."

Samuel grinned and gave her an enormous hug. "Why do you love me so much, Mommy?"

"Because you're special," she said. "I've looked forward to the time we'll have together while your sisters are away at school. You're a gift from God, and I get to be your mom."

That's what moms do—they choose their children.

The Heart of the Home

Forest Witcraft, administrator for the Boy Scouts, gave us this word of wisdom about priorities:

A hundred years from now it will not matter what my bank account was, the sort of house I lived in, or the kind of car I drove. But the world may be different because I was important in the life of a child.[14]

What the heart is to the body, the mother is to the home.

Those words, written on a small plaque beside our kitchen sink, had a profound impact on the love of my life and her love of our kids. On difficult days that quotation served as a reminder for Beth that motherhood was a marathon and not a sprint. Its message stands in stark contrast to what society teaches and helps keep things in perspective.

What the heart is to the body, the mother is to the home. You are pumping spiritual lifeblood into your kids every single day with your love, your discipline, and your example of Christlikeness.

The world does not always value the time and energy you invest in your children. But whatever the world might say, motherhood is more than a list of chores or a distraction from the "real" work of a career. It is a high and holy calling, the most important job you'll ever have. It is, in the words of Linda Weber, "a complex, beautiful challenge worthy of everything Mom can give to it."[15]

Investing for the Future

According to Reuters, if a stay-at-home mom could be compensated in dollars rather than personal satisfaction and unconditional love, she'd pull in a cool $138,095 a year. That includes work as "housekeeper, cook, day care teacher, laundry machine operator, van driver, facilities manager, janitor, computer operator, chief executive officer and psychologist"—a ninety-plus-hour work week, on average. A mother who holds a full-time job outside the home would earn an additional $85,939 for the work she does at home.[16]

In light of all moms do, that's probably a bargain. But here's a news flash: don't rush to your laptop to check your bank account. No direct deposits have been made.

In reality, it's the other way around. Mothers are the ones making the deposits—enormous deposits—every single day into their children's spiritual accounts. And a hundred years from now, those investments will still be yielding returns in the lives of children, grandchildren, and great-grandchildren.

Some mothers downplay the significance of their role, saying things like "I'm just a stay-at-home mom" or "I'm an architect—and, oh yes, I have three children at home."

But being a mother isn't a second-rate career. When you're trying to raise kids who love the Lord, the mother's role is incalculable. If you don't understand your value in the eyes of God, how can you see the value in raising godly children? You can't pass on what you don't possess yourself. You are valuable to the Lord, and so are the chores and challenges of motherhood.

You are the heart of the home. Choose to invest yourself wisely.

Choose to Be a Stabilizing Presence

Busyness is the hallmark of the modern world—we're all multitasking, juggling, living fractured, fragmented lives. But busyness is the enemy of peace. A family in chaos, with everybody running off to do their own thing, creates instability and insecurity in a child's heart.

Mom, you're the one who sets the tone in the home. Your home is to be a training ground where spiritual lessons are taught and reinforced. You're the one who can create an atmosphere of acceptance, a place of peace, and an environment of grace and joy.

A key factor in creating this stable atmosphere is the mom's relationship with her husband. Next to your relationship with Christ, your connection with your husband should be top priority . . . even before the children. Children are very perceptive; they learn quickly what type of relationship their parents have. Work on that relationship. Give it the time and attention it needs. Find peace and joy in your relationship, and you'll communicate those to your children.

Don't buy into the current cultural trend of your children being involved in countless activities—it will wear all of you out. Instead, be a calming presence providing structure, so that your kids sense that home is a safe place.

Protect your family time with the tenacity of a Doberman. Give your children breathing room and margin in their life. Choose to say no to countless activities on their behalf, so that you have time to convey lessons to your children, and they have time to absorb them.

Have meals together. Studies show that regular family mealtimes result in better grades, better relationships, better manners, better self-esteem, better health, and fewer behavior problems.[17]

In our house, Beth goes to great lengths to protect dinnertime. We try to eat dinner as a family at least four times a week, but the older the kids get, the more complicated the schedule becomes. Sometimes we end up having dinner at 9:00, but it's worth it to be together. And we are *together*: no phone calls, no e-mails, no texts, no tweets at the table. (Merely typing the phrase causes me to twitch!) Beth's determination is the light that beckons us safely in to port rather than becoming ships that pass in the night.

Sometime ago I was in a home with a family where the mother had allowed her three-year-old daughter to rule the roost. During my short stay the threatening mom would repeatedly say: "You're gonna get a spanking" or "I'm gonna put you in time-out!"

The promised discipline, of course, never materialized. Finally the little girl climbed up and began jumping up and down on the kitchen table. Her mom said, "You better get down before I count to ten!"

Now, I'm not a fan of the "count to three" routine, but . . . *ten*? The kid's got time to rob a bank and return while the mother's still counting!

Well, Mom kept counting and the kid kept jumping. Guess when the princess finally started moving? If you guessed nine, you're pretty close. But it was actually nine *and a half*.

Maybe the mom had in mind teaching her toddler to count—or even learn fractions. But it was a poor way to instill respect within the child and a far cry from first-time obedience.

Moms, you have the God-given authority to lead, direct, and discipline your children. Don't relinquish that responsibility to your six- or sixteen-year-old. Your expectation of obedience will bring order and calm to the home front.

Choose to Be the Voice of Affirmation

We all know that motherhood includes an almost endless list of chores. But the real substance happens in between washing dishes and folding clothes. A mother is there when the child needs a listening ear, a comforting word, a stern glance, a reassuring hug, or a heartfelt prayer.

At least we hope she is.

The mother of entertainer Barbra Streisand passed away several years ago. Their relationship had long been strained. When Barbra had her big comeback concert at Madison Square Garden, her mother was eighty-five years old. Barbra greeted her mother in the second row and asked, "Are you proud of me now, Mama?"[18]

Some of you can probably relate to their strife firsthand. Like Barbra Streisand, you are still waiting and wishing for a blessing from your mom. Some word of affirmation. Any word.

Make the choice. Break the cycle. Don't withhold that gift from your children. We can live in the past, or we can learn from the past. There's no wisdom in repeating the sins of previous generations.

The year I turned sixteen was an awkward time in my life. I grew seven inches in twelve months, and despite my dad's attempts to save money and put off buying me new pants, I didn't believe him when he told me that knickers were coming back in style.

Like most sixteen-year-olds, I struggled with my self-image. I don't know what possessed me, but I decided to run for senior class president of my school. My mom realized that this campaign was a vulnerable risk for a kid to take.

The day of the election, I came home to find an enormous sign on the front door of the house. It said, "Win or lose—we love you!"

With those simple words, my mother communicated an important message to an awkward adolescent: *Regardless of what others may think of you, within these four walls you will always be a winner.* As a result, I didn't have to go through life wondering to myself, *Are you proud of me now, Mama?*

And, yes, I won. But the outcome didn't matter half as much as knowing I was loved unconditionally. Whether I won or lost, my mom would always choose me.

Choose to Create Teachable Moments

When the kids were young, Beth was always looking for a way to teach them to focus on others. She constantly talked to them about the nine qualities of the fruit of the Spirit. Then she came up with a brilliant idea. She made a special fruit of the Spirit plate, and she would select one member of our family as "the special one" for the evening. We'd each pray and thank God for that family member and then specifically name what fruit of the Spirit we had recently observed in him or her. It became a time of commending one another and creating a memory that reinforced their positive actions toward others.

Our friend Haylie conceived of another creative way to generate teachable moments. She saves the Christmas cards their family receives and keeps them in a basket near the table. On the nights when they eat together at home, they thank God for their food, but they also pull a Christmas card out of the basket and pray for that family.

Choose to Encourage the Faith

Remember Hannah? She desperately wanted a baby but couldn't conceive. So she went into the temple and asked God to give her a child.

God did. And then Hannah did something remarkable: she gave her son back to the Lord.

"I prayed for this child," she said, "and the LORD has granted me what I asked of him. So now I give him to the

We can live
in the past, or
we can learn
from the past.

LORD. For his whole life he will be given over to the LORD" (1 Samuel 1:27–28).

Motherhood is a partnership with God. It involves helping shape the next generation for a lifetime of representing Christ. Hannah gave her son to God, and young Samuel became one of Israel's greatest prophets.

Beth takes that partnership seriously. When we don't know how best to handle a situation, she asks for wisdom. She prays for our children every day. She seeks God to help her understand what is going on in the hearts of our kids. The Lord may reveal His wisdom to Beth through something she reads, a conversation with someone, or a creative idea for teaching spiritual principles to our children.

Offer your children back to God. Hold them up in prayer. Help guide them in determining God's plan. You may want to try and lead your teenage children through the exercise of choosing a life verse. Help them locate and learn a Scripture verse that summarizes their beliefs and pursuits. Help them think about how the principles of godly living apply to their everyday lives. Show them by example what it means to love the Lord their God with all their heart and soul and mind and strength.

Choose to Replenish Your Soul

One of the best things you can do for your children is to keep your own spiritual reservoirs full. You can stretch in so many horizontal directions that you neglect the vertical one—your connection with the Lord.

But you can't give what you don't possess. As Angela Thomas said:

> Mothering requires everything. But eventually, everything given *plus* little replenished *equals* desperately empty. I held the empty cup of my soul out to my husband and begged him to fill it. I held out my cup to a bigger house. . . . But only Jesus could fill my soul. I tried my children and my girlfriends, but again, they could not fill the place designed by God for Himself. . . . I had been mistaken. I thought that the goal of motherhood was to be a Supermom. But in fact, the goal of mothering is to be a woman of God to your children.[19]

God's Word for All Sorts of Moms

Maybe you have a blended family, and your kids are only with you some of the time. Then pray for the "other" mom to water the seeds you plant in your children.

Maybe you're a single mom in need of spiritual support. Then find hope and support in Psalm 68:5, where the Lord is described as "a father to the fatherless." There's no better partner you could hope to have, imparting His Spirit and comfort to those who don't have a dad.

Maybe you're a working mom, and you feel a little guilty about the limited time you have with your children. Then listen to the words of author Linda Weber, whose mother worked outside the home:

> Mom worked at outside jobs. She had to. But Mom understood the importance of giving her *best* efforts to what was most important—her children. . . . Though Mom didn't give us a high standard of living, she gave us a high standard of life.[20]

God will help you become godly. A woman of God is intimately connected to her Savior. A woman of God can love and give from the overflowing cup God has filled.

Be intentional about showing your children what it means to love God and respect His Word. Trust that He can make you a better parent. Fight the tendency to speed up the parenting process. If you're too focused on completing the task, you may miss out on both the moments and the meaning of motherhood.

Our kids don't have a "pause" button; we can't put them on hold while we figure out what's really important in life. Helen Young reminds us of this in *Children Won't Wait*:

There will be a time when there will
be no slamming of doors
No toys on the stairs, no childhood quarrels,
no fingerprints on the wallpaper.
Then may I look back with joy and not regret.
God, give me the wisdom to see that
today is my day with my children.
That there is no unimportant moment in their lives.
May I know that no other career is so precious,
No other work so rewarding,
No other task so urgent.
May I not defer it nor neglect it,
But by the Spirit accept it gladly, joyously,
and by Thy grace realize
That the time is short and my time is now,
For children won't wait.[21]

Being a mother is not just about being chief cook, taxi driver, housekeeper, dog-walker, kisser of boo-boos, and bandager of knees and elbows. It's about investing yourself in your relationship with God and passing that on to your sons and daughters. Your children need to know how special they are to you—more important than any possession or promotion. You are also the vital link in the chain of faith which passes down from generation to generation.

Right now, today, you are choosing to give your kids what they need to trust God, to venture out on their own, and to allow God to write His story in their lives.

Choose your children.

It's a choice you'll never regret. Because a hundred years from now, when you've gone to be with Jesus, your mother's heart will still be beating in the hearts of children and grandchildren and great-grandchildren who love and serve the Lord.

7

A Father's Gifts

Becky seemed to work more diligently on her family picture than any of her other kindergarten classmates. She wanted it to be perfect. After all, this was going to be imprinted on a plate, taken home, and cherished forever. With the focus of a surgeon, Becky carefully drew a picture of herself beside her mom and the family dog. She included every detail, even drawing the little baby inside Mom's belly. In Becky's mind, the picture was complete.

The drawing was soon etched onto the plate, and Becky proudly took it home. There was only one problem: Becky's parents were not divorced. Becky's mother wasn't a single mom. "But that's how she saw our family," her father Ron says. "I was working so many hours that I wasn't even in the picture."

Twenty-five years later, Ron still has that plate. It reminds him that dads need to be intentional about being involved in the lives of their children.

Get in the Picture

D o you want to be in the picture with your kids? Don't fall for the lie that says they'll naturally grow up to love the Lord with or without your involvement. A father's positive presence and parental participation are huge factors in raising children who love the Lord.

Huge.

If you're a dad reading this book instead of watching ESPN or trading stocks on the Internet, good for you. If you're a mom whose husband is always glued to the TV, the computer, or the work he's brought home from the office, encourage him to read this brief chapter.

Most fathers want to be involved. We want to be good role models and positive influences in our children's lives. We want to affirm and support and love our kids. We just don't always know how.

All dads feel a great deal of pressure. You probably have moments when you feel you are totally in over your head, nights when you can't draw an easy breath. Here's something you might want to know: those feelings of inadequacy are a relief to the Lord. A know-it-all attitude gets in

A father's positive presence and parental participation are huge factors in raising children who love the Lord.

the way of God's work, but a recognition of your need for help opens the door for the Lord to step in.

There's no map or GPS for parenthood; you might as well admit that, sooner or later, you're going to have to ask for directions.

Six Gifts Your Kids Need from You

Dads, there are some things only you can give your kids. And I'm not talking about basketball shoes or cell phones or bigger allowances or expensive vacations. These are gifts much more important than that—and much more valuable. Give your children these gifts, and you will reap the benefits for years to come. Withhold them, and you take the chance of watching helplessly as they head down the wrong road.

Gift #1—Love Their Mom

Remember how it felt when you were dating, before you got married, before the kids came along? Remember how your heart raced when she came into the room? Remember how desperate you were to get her attention? You spent hours thinking about her, writing notes and letters and maybe even poems, trying to sweep her off her feet and show her how much you cared.

Do it again.

Communicate regularly and lovingly with your wife—especially in front of the children. Keep your disputes or arguments private. Take an interest in her interests, do unexpected things for her, treat her the way you did when you were pursuing her. You may think that romancing your wife has little to do with fatherhood, but it is key to helping your children feel safe and loved.

Block out a night once or twice a month for a date night with your wife—just the two of you. I know, I know. You think you're too busy or it's too expensive. But it's an investment you can't afford *not* to make. If you have small children and can't pay a babysitter, find another couple and trade off watching each other's children once a month. Trust me, it will breathe life into the two of you. Both you and your children will benefit.

When our kids were very young, Beth and I would be getting ready for a date night. I'd start speaking in glowing terms to the kids about my plans for the night. They would run back and forth reporting to Beth any secret nuggets about the activities of the evening. Eventually, one of them would look up at me and beg, "Can I go with you?"

My answer was always the same: "No way. I have a date with the most beautiful woman in the world and *you* are not invited."

Does that sound cold or unloving? It wasn't. It was a blessing, a benediction. It gave each of them just what they needed—a sense of security and assurance. Later that night when the babysitter would tuck them into bed, they would fall asleep knowing, "My mommy loves my daddy, and my daddy loves my mommy."

When you are a child, that's a pretty healthy way to end your day.

Love your wife and show it. The best way to be a good father is to be a good husband.

Gift #2—Teach Your Kids Respect

Part of the growing-up process is to test boundaries: to see how much you can get away with; to see where the lines are drawn. Your children will push back. You need to be clear about what's expected of them. Teaching them respect begins in the early years, and it must be reinforced by both parents.

Don't believe it? See how fast your preschooler will go ask Daddy when Mommy says no.

Teach them simple lessons to undergird the importance of respect:

- Look people in the eyes when you speak to them
- The universe doesn't revolve around you
- Express thanks with a grateful heart
- Dive in and serve
- Respond with obedience the first time you're asked
- Treat your mother with respect and honor

Parents can be great at making excuses for their children's lack of respect: "She's shy," "He didn't get much sleep last night," or "He's only thrown a temper tantrum twice this morning—so he's improving."

Well, maybe that's all true, but the bottom line is, you get what you expect. Set the bar high, and when they don't rise to it, administer appropriate consequences. Inherently your children want to please you, so start early teaching them respect for themselves, for others, for property, and for God.

Dad, show some backbone. You may be able to stand up to the board of directors of your $50-million company, but that won't count for much if you can't stand up to your seven-year-old when he back talks his mother, or to your teenage daughter when she starts to leave the house wearing something inappropriate.

Pour into your son a respect for the opposite sex: show basic courtesy and honor to a female of any age. You are his model. Show him by example how women should be treated. Teach your daughter never to accept disrespectful or controlling attitudes. If she sees gentleness and respect in you, she won't tolerate being mistreated by boys.

Gift #3—Make Some Memories with Your Kids

I have a friend who starts every morning at her favorite coffee shop. "It's more than just a great cup of coffee," she says. "It's a place where people talk to one another and community forms, a setting where connections happen and relationships start. You see the same people every day; they become a part of your routine, part of your life."

We could learn a lot from that coffee shop. We need to make the home a gathering place, a place to connect with our kids.

For fathers, the relationship with a son may feel easier because we share common interests. But we need to cultivate a connection with our daughters as well in order to usher them into a well-adjusted adulthood. If the father-daughter relationship is forced or absent, the result may be inferiority, fear, and a lack of discipline.

Research has shown that a daughter who doesn't have a close relationship with her father has a far higher chance of sexual experimentation.[22] She has an innate need for male attention, and God intended for her to get it first from you, Dad. If she doesn't feel loved and needed and secure with her father, she'll go somewhere else.

When my girls were very young, God impressed on me that daughters needed to be cherished by their fathers. I'll admit that the voice sounded suspiciously like my wife, but it was God speaking nevertheless. And they were both right. I made an intentional investment in the lives of my daughters, and I've never regretted the cost or the effort.

Get in the picture. Create traditions together as a family. Don't allow time or money to become an excuse. Let's be honest, you will spend the money on something, so why not

A daughter who doesn't have a close relationship with her father has a far higher chance of sexual experimentation.

invest in activities that will deepen your family bond? Your effort to create memories will make a lasting impression.

Years ago I decided that I wanted to take each of my children on a separate trip to New York City during their teen years. To pull it off meant saving money for a long time. Savannah and I had a special talk in Central Park. Sadie and I held hands and ice-skated together at Rockefeller Plaza. Sam and I went to the all-star game at Yankee Stadium, and we each caught a ball in Home Run Derby. They'd all tell you, and so would I, that these are priceless memories and worth every penny.

But you don't have to go into debt to make memories. Maybe you can start a tradition, an annual activity around a holiday. It might be a spur-of-the-moment surprise, game night or movie night, a trip to see Christmas lights, tubing on the river, or a Memorial Day cookout. Making memories doesn't have to cost a lot. It just has to be a priority.

Little things go a long way with any son or daughter. When the kids were young, about once every six weeks I would take each child, separately, to their "special place" for dinner. This restaurant became a *sacred secret* which they did not disclose to their siblings.

When my daughter, Sadie, was nine, Applebee's® was her special place. She loved to eat the barbecue ribs Kid's Meal. Once after Sadie and I returned from eating together, six-year-old Sam got in a close conversation with his sister. He loudly declared, "Sadie, you ate at Applebee's."

Like Simon Peter, she denied it three times. Unconvinced, Sam came over to me and whispered, "Dad, her breath *smells* like Applebee's."

Busted.

Make memories with each of your children. In years to come, they won't remember what you spent. They'll remember what you did.

Gift #4—Give Spiritual Direction to Your Family

A father is without question the single most significant influence on the spiritual life of his children. The statistical data from three major studies in recent years is overwhelming. If the father is involved in a church and is growing spiritually, the likelihood of the child doing the same skyrockets. If Mom goes to church alone with the kids, the chances plummet.

Numbers don't lie:

> If a child is the first person in a household to become a Christian, there is a 3.5 percent probability everyone else in the household will follow. If the mother is the first to become a Christian, there is a 17 percent probability everyone else in the household will follow. But if the father is first, there is a 93 percent probability everyone else in the household will follow.[23]

Is that astounding? Does it put a lump in your throat to realize how important you are in this process?

Men, your kids' pathway to God runs straight through you. If you roll your eyes when prayer is mentioned, so will your children. If you close your eyes and speak of how dependent you are on God for His power and grace, your kids will be more apt to include prayer in their lives.

Read God's Word regularly. Share with your kids what God is teaching you.

Be involved in a church. Be your wife's biggest encourager. Talk to God and ask for His wisdom in parenting.

Tammy's mother taught Sunday school, and the kids always went with her. Their dad would wait in the car and go in for the church service only. One day the kids were complaining and resisting. "Daddy doesn't have to go," they said. "Why do we?"

"My dad overheard our conversation," Tammy said, "and the very next week he started going to Sunday school. That was thirty-five years ago, and to the best of my knowledge he's never missed."

Little eyes are watching. Little ears are listening. As Albert Schweitzer said, "Example is not the main thing in influencing others. It is the only thing."[24]

If you want to produce the real thing, you must be the real thing.

Gift # 5—Encourage Your Kids

Your children need to know that you are in their corner. We are all busy and pulled in a lot of directions, but when your son or daughter takes the stage, the court, or the field, that glance into the crowd is a subtle search for significance. Your absence deflates them. Your presence shouts that they have value. They can pick your voice out of a crowd with the precision of a piano tuner.

Christian author John Eldredge says, "Your son or daughter, no matter how old, will always want and need to hear those words from you. 'You have what it takes . . . You are worth fighting for.'"[25]

Your positive comments and attitude help shape your children's self-esteem. Affirm them. Let them know you're proud. Let your daughter know that you think she's beautiful and smart, talented and capable. Catch your son doing something right and commend him in front of others.

Dads play a key role in determining whether children venture outside their comfort zone or fearfully settle for a status quo existence. Your genuine affirmation provides a safety net for taking risks and stretching their confidence.

Gift #6—Invest Quality Time

In this frantic world, time has become the most precious commodity. But it's not just time that's important—it's quality time, attentive time. Sometimes I am with my family, but my mind is elsewhere. Later my wife will say to me: "Well, Dave, you were there—but you weren't *there*." And although I am slow to admit it, I know she's right.

We need to stop seeing busyness as a badge of honor. We may be "important" people with "important" things to do, but the end result is always the same for our families. They get what we men tend to complain about: the leftovers.

At one time in my life, I was enjoying the climb rather than focusing my attention and priorities on my wife and small children. The ministry, like any other profession, can eat you alive if you let it. I gave at the office—sixty-hour weeks like an obsessed and driven workaholic. My self-imposed quest to provide for my family was actually causing me to neglect them.

Like my friend Ron, I was out of the family picture.

All that changed one Father's Day. Before my sermon a soloist sang a song with this refrain:

> *Slow down, Daddy, don't work so hard.*
> *We're proud of our house, we've got a big enough yard.*
> *Slow down, Daddy—we want you around—*
> *Daddy, please slow down.*[26]

When she finished singing, I went to the pulpit to preach. I opened my mouth, but no words came out. The emotion and guilt left me speechless. The congregation had to sing a chorus so that I could regain my composure.

Our Children's Ministry director, Linda Brandon, happened to be in that particular service with her young son. He turned to her and said, "Mommy, why is Mr. Stone crying?"

Dad's play a key role in determining whether children venture outside their comfort zone or fearfully settle for a status quo existence.

Linda candidly replied, "Well, when the Holy Spirit convicts you of sin in your life, sometimes you cry."

Ouch! (Don't hold back, Linda, tell me how you really feel. . . .)

I can laugh about it now, but you know what? She was 100 percent right. God used the words of that song as a wake-up call. With the Lord's help, I changed. I put my family back on the priority list.

Ever since then, I've been in the picture. Sometimes a little fuzzy and out of focus, but there. And I plan to stay there. Forever.

Dads, be encouraged. You *can* do this. You really can . . . just not on your own. Invite the Lord and your wife into the equation. From this point forward, things can be different. Things can be better.

Check your priorities. Be intentional.

Slow down. Step up.

Get in the picture.

When you look back years from now, both you and your family will be glad you did.

8

Sharing the Load

Herman Ostry, a farmer in Bruno, Nebraska, bought a piece of land with a barn on it. Shortly after the purchase, a nearby creek flooded, leaving twenty-nine inches of water in Ostry's barn. Half-jokingly, he said to his family, "I bet if we had enough people, we could pick up that barn and carry it to higher ground."

The joke became a challenge. Ostry's son Mike, an engineer, began to do some calculating. He designed a grid of steel tubing to stabilize the inside of the barn. He figured that the barn and stabilizers together weighed approximately 19,000 pounds. If each person lifted around 55 pounds, it would only take 344 people to carry the barn to higher ground.

And then he just had to find 344 people who wouldn't think he was crazy.

On July 30, 1988, the day the town of Bruno celebrated its centennial, 344 people gathered around the Ostrys' barn. As thousands watched, Herman counted, "One, two, three . . ."

The barn rose from its foundation. The crowd cheered as they carried over nine tons of structure fifty yards up a hill in just three minutes.[27]

How did they do it? Everyone shared a common goal. The load was evenly distributed. There were no superstars. As a team they all moved in the same direction. And together they accomplished the impossible.

As parents, we face a seemingly impossible task, raising children to love the Lord and avoid the pitfalls of this world. So why not lighten the load and pull in some other positive influences to help with the heavy lifting?

The more people you involve, the better the chance you have of succeeding.

Painful Parenting

Like it or not, in your kid's eyes, there will come a time when your "coolness" will evaporate. The little girl who proudly held her daddy's hand enters middle school and dreads being seen with her father at a movie theater on a Friday night. The snuggly eight-year-old boy who kisses his mommy and says, "I love you" begins to question if he even *likes* her!

Those transitions wound us. But if we're completely honest, we have to admit that sometimes we feel the same way. That little bundle of joy can morph into a bundle of frustration almost overnight. And you wonder, *Where did I go wrong, and what can I do about it—quick!*

Mark Twain allegedly said, "When your child turns thirteen, stick him in a barrel, place a lid on top, and feed him through the knothole. When he turns sixteen, seal up the knothole!"

Maybe Mark Twain didn't say it at all—although no one recalls seeing any of his children after the eighth grade. But it's worth repeating nevertheless. So if you are a novice parent . . .

Consider yourself forewarned: the barn will get heavier. As an old Yiddish proverb declares, "Little children, little joys; bigger children, bigger sorrows."[28]

The weight of raising a family increases as the years go on. You may not believe it when they're still cute and cuddly, but trust me, there will come a time when your kids refuse to believe you have anything worthwhile to say. But here's the good news: they may still listen to others who share your same values. Be on the lookout for people who can reinforce to your children the importance of making wise, godly choices. Having others close by who are willing to grab a handle and help carry the load can be a welcome relief—and their help allows you to catch your breath.

And in the meantime you may be that positive influence in the life of someone else's children. Has your SUV become the resident shuttle service for the neighborhood? Are you coaching a soccer or softball team? Is your kitchen the place the kids hang out after school? Embrace the opportunity. Seize the moment and make wise deposits into their young lives. Give what you have to offer to other kids who are in need and trust that the Lord will put some positive influences in front of *your* kids.

Spiritual Role Models

When our son Sam was starting middle school, we hosted a weekly Bible study in our home for thirty or so college-age guys and gals. During that time, we chose to have our son stay home instead of attend his youth program at church. It was a formative time in Sam's life, and at the Bible study he had the chance to be exposed to some remarkable Christian role models.

In the process, we discovered that it does wonders for a kid's self-image to have college students and young adults take an interest in his everyday life. It made Sam feel special and gave him confidence in who he was and who he might become.

Since they stayed late and Sam had an early bedtime, some Wednesdays I would send one of the young men upstairs to Sam's room to pray with him. It gave them practice for the future when they might have children of their own. It also deepened the bond Sam had with these guys he revered.

One night I sent Chris Burke up to pray with Sam. A few minutes later Chris returned downstairs. "Well, I just made a fool of myself," he admitted. "I said to Sam, 'So what exactly do you all do when you pray?'

"From his bed, Sam just looked up at me and in a real matter-of-fact voice, said, 'Well, Chris, we talk to God.'"

Chris turned a bright shade of red. "Dave, what I was asking is 'What's the format of how you do this?'"

"Sure you were," I said.

We never let him live it down.

Spiritual role models may be neighbors or relatives, coaches or teachers, babysitters or grandparents. All that matters is that they are people who share your commitment to the Lord, positive individuals who appreciate your children's uniqueness, realize their potential, and want to help them grow spiritually.

Grandparents

I'm often asked, "Why is it so natural for grandparents and grandchildren to get along?"

And my answer is always the same: "That's easy! They share a *common enemy*!"

But seriously, grandparents are an often-overlooked source of spiritual support. They have a vested interest in seeing the family name and reputation go on. In most cases they are willing to make huge sacrifices of time to have the chance to impact your children. And they usually love doing it. With a little encouragement, they can become a teacher to your toddler and a sounding board for your teen.

When I talk to people who have just joined our church, I'll ask them to tell me about their earliest memory of church. One of the most common responses is that a grandparent used to go out of the way to take them to church.

If your parents share your spiritual values and goals, you've got a valuable resource at your disposal. One your children will respond to even when it seems they no longer listen to a word you say.

Babysitters

The babysitter is another formative influence in the lives of your children. The people you hire to look after your kids when you can't be there are more than just caregivers. They are role models, both spiritually and socially. They can help reinforce whatever lessons or habits you are working on with your children, and they may also demonstrate how a Christian navigates through growing up, dating, and courtship.

About once a year Beth and I go on a trip that requires us to be gone for several days. We always try to find a young single woman or a sharp young couple who are exemplary models of genuine faith to stay with our kids.

We want our children to see that type of commitment as normal and achievable.

When I was a kid, my parents would ask our favorite youth coaches at church to stay with us. My brother and I didn't think our parents were *cool*, but in those middle-school years, Tom and Linda Wicks certainly qualified. Some of my best memories are times with Tom and Linda—going out for pizza, showing them my makeshift high jump pit in the backyard, and cooking popcorn together.

Show Me Your Friends

Todd Clark, who was our student minister years ago, said to our youth, "Show me your friends and I'll show you your future."

That statement may bring great relief or create fear and trembling, but know this—it's the truth. The apostle Paul issued a similar warning: "Bad company corrupts good character" (1 Corinthians 15:33).

Your children's friendships will determine the direction of their faith. If I could pray only one thing for my kids, it wouldn't be for intelligence or beauty or athleticism. It wouldn't be for an easy life or a good education or a profitable job. It wouldn't even be for their future spouse or children.

If I could pray only one thing, it would be that God would surround them with friends who love the Lord.

When your children are small, you need to influence the selection of their closest friends. You have to help guide them to the kids who'll become their playmates and buddies. If you do it early, it will set a pattern for them to choose wisely as they get older.

Play your cards right, and you can have some say in whom they'll want to imitate. Put them in settings where they will have older kids to look up to spiritually. While your children may *listen* to you, at times they will *look* to other role models for encouragement.

Just make sure they're looking in the right direction.

The summer of my sophomore year in college, I volunteered to work at a week of church camp. One of the campers was Charlie, a high school boy who was extremely popular and loved by everyone. On Thursday night we had a campfire service. The sermon was over, and we were all getting ready to leave when Charlie stood up and started crying.

"I feel like God is calling me to change the direction of my life," he said. He reached in his pocket and pulled out a bag of marijuana. "I came to this week at camp with some really impure motives. I'm going to turn my life over to Christ."

And with that he took the marijuana and threw it in the campfire.

Are you thinking what I was thinking?

Let me just say, they don't prepare you for this in Bible college. We quickly dismissed the kids to their bunks. Some of the faculty thought that the week had gone to pot. I chose to look at it more as a spiritual high!

(Just in case you are wondering—no, you can't get a buzz from the smell of marijuana no matter how hard you try.)

Charlie's spiritual rededication was the first of many that week. His parents put him in an environment where he could see some older, positive role models and hear biblical truth. And Charlie discovered—as many of the campers did—that God specializes in second chances. Camp allowed him to be around some different kids and adults. New friends were helping him start to shape a new future.

The Most Influential Influencer

Throughout our parenting years, God has brought quality Christian role models into the paths of our children, not because we were *special*, but because we were *intentional*. Whenever we met new people, our antennae went up for potential spiritual influencers who could impact our kids. We wanted to involve as many committed believers as we possibly could, to surround our kids with caring Christians. We were always on the lookout for family and friends who could influence our children and fortify our commitment to bring them up to love the Lord. Whether it was Erica the babysitter or Chris the athlete, our kids' confidence and faith grew. As a result of these special people's investment of time, our kids' future looks brighter.

But here's the crux of the matter: It wasn't our efforts that made the biggest difference. It was God's grace.

Go ahead. Reinforce the barn. Surround your children with people who are willing to help lift the load and carry them to higher ground. Get other people involved in their lives—older kids, babysitters, youth leaders, coaches, teachers, counselors, grandparents, anyone who can offer a different voice and a godly perspective. Be aware of and thankful for those influencers who are prompted and used by the Divine to help make a difference in the next generation.

Just don't neglect to thank the most influential Influencer.

In the final analysis, God is the One who is truly responsible. If our kids grow up to love the Lord, it won't be because of our exceptional parenting skills or our self-appointed lineup of friends, relatives, and mentors.

It will be because the compass of God's Spirit steers our kids in the right direction. God and God alone is the One who draws our children to Him.

By ourselves, it's futile.

With others, there's a chance.

But with God, all things are possible . . . whether you are raising a barn or a baby.

9

The Spittin' Image

Dave, who do you think the baby looks like?"

An awkward silence follows. You might call it a *pregnant* pause.

Now, I have a few talents: Ping-Pong, juggling, golf, and standing on my head for two minutes. But if I show up in the maternity ward, please don't ask me to determine who your baby looks like. God did not bless me with the gift of deciphering facial features.

You might argue that, statistically, I've got a fifty-fifty chance of getting it right. But that's not my experience. If I say, "He looks like his mother," everyone in the room will chuckle, and my wife will quickly say, "Look again. He's got his daddy's chin."

At that moment I'm thinking to myself, *Their chins look nothing alike. His dad has a goatee.*

Shows how much I know.

I do know this, though: Winston Churchill had it right when he said, "All babies look like me."

But not forever. Time passes, little Jackson goes through his growth spurt, and fills out, and years later it's a different story. He walks across the room, turns to his friend and smiles, and suddenly it's all there. The eyes, the smile, the chin—he's the spittin' image of his father.

The Image of the Father

It's an odd choice of words, isn't it? "The spittin' image."

Some sources claim that the phrase refers to a child displaying both the internal qualities of the parents (the spit) and the physical likeness (the image). Others believe the expression is a corruption of "spirit and image"—a child is identified as the "spirit and image" of the father or mother.

Either way, it's a spiritual goal worthy of our effort—to reflect the qualities and likeness of our heavenly Father and to pass that "spirit and image" on to our children.

But that raises the question: how closely do you resemble your heavenly Father? Is the similarity obvious to those around you? As a parent, you have been handed a position and privilege that allows you to shape your child's view of God. If your life doesn't reflect the character of the Lord you claim to follow, then don't bet the farm that your kids' will. But if the image of God is evident in you, it'll be easier for your kids to follow in your footsteps of faith.

Generosity Teaches Selflessness

We're born with a sin nature, and the world around us teaches us to look out for number one. If you don't believe it, set your two-year-old down in a group of toddlers and tell her to share her toys. You'll quickly hear that familiar battle cry from her precious little mouth: "Mine! Mine, mine, MINE!"

But what if, through our modeling, our children's first response were to share or give to others?

The biblical principle is clear. The kind of sacrifice God approves is one of justice and generosity:

Is it not to share your food with the hungry
and to provide the poor wanderer with shelter—
when you see the naked, to clothe them,
and not to turn away from your own flesh and blood?
(Isaiah 58:7 NIV 2011).

In his Acts 20:35 sermon Paul told us that Jesus said, "It is more blessed to give than to receive." And we've got a lot to give. By any standard in the world, we are wealthy people. We can hoard that wealth, or we can be generous with it, but whatever we do, our kids will imitate.

Years ago Beth and I started a tradition during our family vacations. We would save and set aside a certain amount of money daily to be given to others as a means of encouragement. We would pray for God to send someone across our path, someone in need of a small dose of hope, encouragement, or money. Sometimes it took some convincing that there were no strings attached.

This was at a time when we didn't have much—five or ten dollars was our ice cream money. But even when they were very young, our children understood that giving up ice cream might help somebody else have their first meal in a week. The spontaneous hugs they received or the occasional tear they observed propelled them to continue to be generous to others. They learned the joy of generosity.

John 3:16 begins with this simple phrase, "For God so loved the world that he *gave* . . ." (emphasis added). Generosity models for your children how to hold the things of this world loosely. This goes against the grain of our culture. But the goal isn't to *have* more; it's to *give* more. Generosity feeds a spirit that focuses on others more than self. When your kids learn that it's more blessed to give than to receive, they will experience the addictive thrill of giving.

One of the best ways to look more like God is to look less like the world.

And we never look more like God than when we give.

Availability Fuels Communication

Relationships can't flourish without connection. Jesus knew this, but apparently His disciples had gotten things confused—again. In Matthew 19, the disciples go into Secret Service mode and won't allow kids to get close to Jesus. He gently rebukes His peers and basically says, "Let the little children come to me . . . for the kingdom of heaven belongs to such as these" (v. 14).

Take time for your children. Be available and accessible, as God is available and accessible for you.

I grew up in a preacher's home. My father was busy with a demanding schedule, but he always made time for family. One day my dad received a telephone call from the preacher of a large, well-known church. As I listened from the other room, it was obvious Dad was being asked to come and speak. His excitement was evident. "February 3? I'd love to. First let me check my calendar."

He went bounding up the stairs to get his calendar, and as he did, my heart sank. February 3rd was the night of a program at my middle school, and I had a significant part in it.

Dad returned to the kitchen wall phone, and flipped through the pages of his appointment booklet. At last I heard him say, "February 3rd? No, I'm sorry, but I already have a commitment on that evening. Maybe some other time."

Without saying a single word to me, he communicated his availability, love, and support. *I* was his commitment, and nothing could entice him away from an appointment with his son.

In that availability, I saw God.

Repentance Leads to Forgiveness

God the Father specializes in redeeming our mistakes. That's who He is and what He does. But the prelude to forgiveness is repentance.

Sometimes people think that confession and repentance are the same thing. Both are good and necessary, but confession is with the mouth and repentance is with the heart. Repentance literally means an about-face, a 180-degree turn, a change of direction. Acts 3:19 says, "Repent, then, and turn to God."

Sometimes kids will get caught red-handed and say, "I'm sorry." But lots of times that's regret, not repentance. There's no remorse over the disobedience, merely over the fact that they were caught in the act.

In those instances we would send our kids to their room to think and pray about their offense. They had to stay there until they were ready to "make it right." From the age of three on, they were expected to make it right with God and with the person they'd offended. Their apology had to be specific, stating what they'd done.

When they would say, "But I didn't do anything wrong!" we would ask them to go to their room and ask God to reveal to them what they did wrong. Sometimes they would emerge prematurely, but a casual, halfhearted "Sorry!" would result in the "opportunity" to spend more time praying and thinking about it.

Give it a try. Let God speak to your children. You may find that the tenderhearted ones will apologize within three minutes, while the firstborns stay in their room 'til the Second Coming! But don't lose the battle of the wills. When we sin, whether we are eight or eighty, we wound God and offend His holiness. Our job as parents is to reach our children's hearts and teach them that their earthly parents and their heavenly Parent will forgive the repentant.

Back when my daughter Sadie was nine, she talked disrespectfully to me as I was putting her to bed. I told her that she needed to think about it and pray about it. I reminded her that she had the Holy Spirit living inside of her and He would show her what she needed to do. I said, "I know you will choose to make it right."

More than an hour went by. I waited in my room for her to apologize, but she didn't come and didn't come. Finally I realized that she had fallen asleep.

About three in the morning, Beth and I awakened to Sadie standing by our bed. "It's not morning yet. Go back to sleep," we said and quickly sent her back to her room. Early the next morning, while I was still asleep, Beth was up making breakfast when Sadie straggled in.

"Sadie," she asked, "did you have a bad dream last night?"

"No," Sadie said. "I woke up and I couldn't go back to sleep until I could make it right with Daddy."

That's the difference between regret and repentance. It's a good feeling for them, for you, and for God when they make it right. And it establishes a pattern that will get them in the habit of making it right with God throughout adolescence and adulthood.

Even when they wake you out of a dead sleep to do it.

Serving Together Deepens Faith

A long-term, extensive study was conducted of numerous students to determine who was likely to stay in a faith community as they move from adolescence into adulthood. It's no surprise that the more deeply the teens were woven into the fabric of the congregation through activities and involvement, the more likely they were to continue on that path in the adult years.

The results were summarized in *The Journal of Youth Ministry*:

Those who want to help young people develop a

rigorous, meaningful faith life should involve them in meaningful service. . . . Treating teenagers as partners in ministry rather than objects of ministry is an important and empowering distinction for developing new generations of spiritual leaders.[29]

The single biggest "sticky" factor for faith taking root in children is the experience of serving alongside their parents. It may be baking cookies for a neighbor, a spring-break mission trip with "The Fam," or canvassing your neighborhood and picking up trash.

What you choose to do isn't important.

Who you do it with is.

Why? Because serving gets you out of your comfort zone, and it can be quite humbling. Getting your hands dirty removes the layers of pretension and pride which so many *spectator* Christians have.

When you serve, you start to look like Jesus. The King of the universe left heaven and came to Earth to wash feet and touch lepers. It's a riches-to-rags story if there ever was one. In an effort to model the way for His disciples, Jesus washed their feet. He said, "For even the Son of Man did not come to be served, but to serve, and to give his life as a ransom for many" (Mark 10:45).

Some of my greatest memories with my family revolve around service. Together we worked on a Habitat for Humanity home. We served Thanksgiving meals for three days in a parking lot following Hurricane Katrina. With my two youngest, we shared food with a group of homeless people with whom we'd eat, laugh, and pray.

Every act of service your family does together will bear fruit in your offspring. Any time you step out of the spotlight and focus on meeting the needs around you, you are modeling for your kids true Christianity.

Authenticity Reflects Godliness

You can teach your children how to repent, but the best lesson they'll learn about forgiveness is when *you* ask them for it. When you blow it, don't be afraid to say to your four-year-old, "Mommy got upset and lost her patience at lunch. I shouldn't have shouted at you. Will you please forgive me?" Say to your teenager, "I was unreasonable with you. I'm sorry." Say to your kids, "I had a hard day and took it out on you. Please forgive me."

Plenty of times I have had to ask forgiveness of my kids. Those are tough moments, but they display that the principles of godly living are true regardless of whether you are the parent or the child.

I remember one night making a joke at my son's expense in front of my Bible study group. These were role models to him. Now, Sam has a great sense of humor, but that night my words crossed the line and went beyond good-natured joking. After a couple of minutes, I saw him slide out of the room. I knew I had wounded him—and it's a terrible feeling. Quickly I expressed my remorse to the group I was leading.

But during my lesson I couldn't get it off my mind. I finally said, "I'm gonna go take care of something, if you'll give me a few minutes." I excused myself from the group and went to find Sam.

He was in his room with his head buried in his pillow. I said, "I owe you an apology. I never should have said that. Will you forgive me?"

He looked at me with red eyes. "You made everyone laugh at me."

I said, "You are so right. I shouldn't have. I blew it. I feel terrible that I hurt you. I apologized to the group, and they forgave me. Will you forgive me and give me another chance?"

My ten-year-old paused and then said, "I forgive you, Dad." I hugged him and I headed downstairs with red eyes to share the good news with the group of young adults. That became the lesson that stuck with them—not the one I'd prepared.

Parents, when we have wronged our children in some way, we need to go to God asking for His forgiveness and go to them asking for their forgiveness as well. When you swallow your pride and do that, you are modeling for them what you hope they will do with you when they disobey or disappoint you. But more importantly, you are showing them what to do when they let God down.

Paul reminded us that "we, who with unveiled faces all reflect the Lord's glory, are being transformed into his likeness with ever-increasing glory, which comes from the Lord, who is the Spirit" (2 Corinthians 3:18). The more we look to Jesus, the more we reflect His likeness.

So keep looking into the mirror until you no longer see yourself, but rather see the spirit and image of Christ. When you reflect that image, you can pass it on to your children. Your kids may or may not bear a physical resemblance to you, but they will bear a spiritual likeness to you.

They'll grow up to be the spittin' image of both their earthly parents and their loving heavenly Father.

And that will be a very good thing.

10

The Last Word

So, how's your Parental Report Card?

Don't deny it. I know you've been doing it. Reading chapter after chapter and grading yourself along the way:

- "I do the prayer thing fairly well."
- "We're not so hot on consistency."
- "I'm improving on spending time with the kids."
- "Compared to Sara, I'm pitiful at encouragement."

It's a roller coaster, isn't it? Sometimes it's a grinding climb upward; sometimes, an exhilarating swoop down and around the curves. It's easy to become negative in the tough times or self-satisfied when things are going well. But here's a warning: Comparison games or beating yourself up for your failures won't help you or your family. Guilt trips don't produce change; they only produce guilt.

That's why we don't call them change trips.

Don't be discouraged. No matter how perfect the family pictures look, every family struggles and is dependent on God's grace and mercy.

Thankfully, we can find some comfort in the Bible itself. Eugene Peterson writes:

> A search of Scripture turns up one rather surprising truth: there are no exemplary families. Not a single family is portrayed in Scripture in such a way so as to evoke admiration in us. . . . The biblical material consistently portrays the family not as a Norman Rockwell group, beaming in gratitude around a Thanksgiving turkey, but as a series of broken relationships in need of redemption.[30]

Evidently God isn't expecting us to be perfect. He just wants us to look to the One who is. If God is truly more concerned with direction than perfection, then next year you'll be a better parent, because you are learning, maturing, and being transformed by His Spirit.

Divine Intervention

While we are in the process of raising our kids, the jury is still out as to whether they will embrace faith for themselves. The true test comes when they leave home. In an environment of freedom, will they stray or stay the course?

Your job is to prepare and pave the way for that transition. But don't miss this: it doesn't all rest on your shoulders. While you do play a pivotal role in the parenting process, you don't have the final say about your child's faith. Believe it or not, neither does your child.

The Lord has the last word.

There will be times when you think the story is complete, moments when you think your teen or college student may be a lost cause. But, in the words of Gracie Allen, "Never place a period where God has placed a comma."[31]

Don't give up. Continue to pray. And remember that God is "able to do immeasurably more than all we ask or imagine" (Ephesians 3:20).

Do not underestimate the difference God can make. Trust Him. His power and presence can affect your parenting more than all your noble efforts. When it comes to raising kids who love the Lord, He specializes in making up the difference.

Some of you may feel like the odds are stacked against you. Maybe you're a single parent. Maybe you have an unbelieving spouse or are facing the challenge of a blended family. Maybe you've spent years pretending to be a spiritual family, or you've started later than you should have on intentional parenting.

Here's the good news: God loves a challenge. You're a perfect candidate for His grace and greater involvement. He's in your corner.

Don't take my word for it.

Ask a slave child named Moses.

Ask a teenage shepherd named David.

Ask an orphan girl named Esther.

Ask a frightened introvert named Gideon.

God understands underdogs. And He cares just as much about you as any person on that list. Invite His participation in your family. The Bible paints a picture of His character and compassion that should prompt us to want His participation in our parenting.

Do your part—and pray that your adult children do theirs. God will do the rest. Trust the Lord: He's faithful. "He who began a good work in you will carry it on to completion" (Philippians 1:6).

All *we* can do is our best. But *God*—now He's a different story. Regardless of the mistakes you've made or the mess in which you find yourself, remember what God does best: He restores. He rebuilds. He redeems.

And He can do that with your family.

God restores.
He rebuilds.
He redeems.
And He can
do that with
your family.

Inside Out

Truly effective parenting comes down to the heart—your heart, your child's heart, and the heart of God. His Spirit can fill in the gaps. So don't give up or grow weary in your daily investment in parenting.

When my oldest child, Savannah, was in the fourth grade, I surprised her and took her to Savannah, Georgia. Her name was everywhere—which is quite exciting when you're nine. Then during her senior year of high school I was invited to Savannah again, to speak at a leadership conference.

I wanted to take Savannah with me.

She was going off to college, and it was evident to both Beth and me that she would most likely marry her boyfriend, Patrick, in the next few years. Opportunities for uninterrupted time for just the two of us were diminishing rapidly.

Fortunately for me, Savannah jumped at the opportunity.

While speaking in my last main session, I shared with this group of Christian leaders the story of the "Slow Down, Daddy" song (the one I tell about in chapter 7). That emotional moment twelve years before had become God's wake-up call to shake me out of some prideful, workaholic patterns. It was a surreal experience to share that defining moment in my life with my college-bound daughter sitting in the audience. But I wondered what was going through *her* mind as she listened.

That afternoon I discovered this on my laptop:

Dear Dad,

Thank you for bringing me back to Savannah. I just wanted to take this chance to tell you how much I appreciate you. It hasn't been until recently that I've realized how much I really watched you and how much you influenced me.

I know we've gone through things—selfish hearts, stubborn minds, etc.—where I haven't shown I've cared, but I hope that from now on, I can show you a lot clearer and a lot more often just how much you mean to me. Spiritually, you helped model a relationship with Christ. Not just through sermons but in everyday life, in the way you handle circumstances, pray for things, seek godly counsel, etc. With Patrick and me, I love how you've reached out to us. You have loved us and taken an interest not just in our relationship, but a genuine interest in Patrick's life. We have so much fun with you and Mom. I know the way that Patrick and I have chosen to do things, pray together, work through problems, and show our love have been pure and glorifying to God because of the example you've been.

When I get married, I know I'll come to realize even more how much wisdom you gave to us and will be able to give me in the future. I hope the man I marry is half the man you are. I'll always be your little girl. This may be one of our last real "Daddy and Daughter" trips, but I'll remember these trips forever. They strengthened our relationship and my relationship with God, introduced me to many people and places, and showed me how special I am to you. So thanks, Dad, for all you've done and will do. Thanks for always thinking of our family when it comes to your priorities. Thanks for "slowing down, Daddy."

I love you,
Savannah

By the time I finished, my cheeks were streaked with tears. I mumbled a "Thank You, Lord," but it's tough to talk with a lump in your throat.

I've often wondered how my story would have played out had I remained on that workaholic path. But thank God, the Holy Spirit got my attention and I listened. He transformed me and my parenting. He can do the same for you.

When I was growing up, my mom was fond of saying that verse 4 of 3 John was her favorite: "I have no greater joy than to hear that my children are walking in the truth."

And I always wondered, *Why would that verse stand out to her?*

I didn't understand then—but I do now.

We all share the same goal that Heather expressed to me that Sunday morning in the church hallway. We want our children to grow up to love the Lord.

So this book ends the same way it began: with an appeal for authenticity. Parents, be real. Your kids need faith, joy, integrity, and authenticity.

Trust God. Trust your family to God. Let the Spirit work in you and through you as you learn to love the Lord and to pass that love on to your children.

And remember, God has the last word. God loves you, and He loves your children. Unconditionally. Consistently. Completely.

God specializes in helping mommies and daddies slow down, be real, and live out the truth of His Word in front of their children. God's goal is the same as yours—to help your family become the family that He wants you to be.

Not a pretend family, not a perfect family—but a family whose kids grow up to love the Lord.

End Notes

1. Jim Gaffigan, Twitter post, July 11, 2011, @JimGaffigan http://twitter.com/#!/JimGaffigan/statuses/90399037659942912

2. Chris Dewelt, from a sermon delivered on July 3, 1997, at the North American Christian Convention in Kansas City, MO.

3. Vance Havner, "Desperation and Revival (1948)," special issue, *The Heartbeat of the Remnant* 14, no. 4 (2008), 23.

4. Senate Chaplain Barry Black, National Day of Prayer Address, Washington, DC, May 6, 2010.

5. John Piper, Twitter post, October 9, 2009, @JohnPiper

6. Erwin McManus, speaking at Group's Ministry Convention, January 18, 2001, Nashville, TN.

7. Dr. Henry Blackaby, speaking at Southeast Christian Church, Louisville, KY, May 15, 2002.

8. "An Hour with J. Russell Morse" interview by Sam E. Stone, *Christian Standard Magazine*, March 4, 1980, 6.

9. Christine Lagorio of CBS News, "Resources: Marketing to Kids" (2009), last accessed September 20, 2012, http://www.cbsnews.com/stories/2007/05/14/fyi/main2798401.shtml.

10. Ross Brodfuehrer, *The Southeast Outlook*, April 4, 2002, A-12.

11. James C. Dobson, *The Strong-Willed Child: Birth through Adolescence* (Carol Stream, IL: Tyndale House, 1992), 29.

12. Josh McDowell and Bob Hostetler, *Josh McDowell's Handbook on Counseling Youth* (Nashville: Thomas Nelson, 1996), 235.

13. Chip Ingram, *Effective Parenting in a Defective World: How to Raise Kids Who Stand Out from the Crowd* (Carol Stream, IL: Tyndale House, 2006), 87.

14. Forest E. Witcraft (1894–1967), Boy Scout Administrator. First published in *Scouting Magazine*, October 1950.

15. Linda Weber, *Mom, You're Incredible* (Colorado Springs: Focus on the Family, 1994), 6.

16. "Stay-at-home mother's work worth $138,095 a year," accessed September 20, 2012, http://www.reuters.com/article/2007/05/02/us-work-mothers-idUSN0236053520070502.

17. "Family Mealtimes: Making an Impact" by Georgia Kostas, posted July 25, 2011, accessed September 20, 2012, http://georgiakostas.wordpress.com/2011/07/25/family-mealtimes-making-an-impact.

18. "Will Yentl Sell?" by Betsy Schiffman, accessed September 20, 2012, http://www.forbes.com/2002/04/12/0412movers.html.

19. Angela Thomas [Guffey], "It's Time to Bench Supermom," *Focus on the Family Magazine*, May 2001.

20. Weber, *Mom, You're Incredible*, 6.

21. Helen M. Young, *Children Won't Wait* (Fort Worth, TX: Brownlow Publishing, 1995).

22. "Devoted dad key to reducing risky teen sex," Linda Carroll, MSNBC Study, last updated 6/5/09, accessed September 20, 2012, http://www.msnbc.msn.com/id/31086977/.

23. "Want your church to grow? Then bring in the men" by Polly House, Baptist Press News (online: posted on April 3, 2003, accessed on September 20, 2012,http://www.bpnews.net/bpnews.asp?id=15630. Statistics from Focus on the Family Publishing, "Promise Keepers at Work."

24. Albert Schweitzer, *Thoughts for Our Times* (White Plains, NY: Peter Pauper Press, 1975), 51.

25. John Eldredge, *You Have What It Takes: What Every Father Needs to Know* (Nashville: Thomas Nelson, 2004), 19.

26. "Slow Down," Words & Music by Bobby Price and Michael James Murphy (Copyright 1991, Tin Roof Music and Riversong Music/SESAC). From the Michael James albums *Shoulder to the Wind* and *Signature Songs*. Used by permission.

27. This story is cited, with some alterations, by Randy Leffingwell, *The American Barn* (Minneapolis: Voyageur Press, 2003), 188. The details I've included are from a direct conversation with Mrs. Ostry in 2003.

28. Kehillat Israel, Reconstructionist Synagogue of Lansing, Michigan.

29. Michael E. Sherr, Diana R. Garland, and Terry A. Wolfer, "The Role of Community Service in the Faith Development of Adolescents," *The Journal of Youth Ministry* 6, no. 1 (Fall 2007): 51.

30. Eugene Peterson, *Like Dew Your Youth: Growing Up with Your Teenager* (Grand Rapids: Eerdmans, 1998), 110.

31. Gracie Allen to George Burns quoted by Peter B. Panagore, *Two Minutes for God: Quick Fixes for the Spirit* (NY: Touchstone/Simon & Schuster: 2007), 73.

Also from Dave Stone

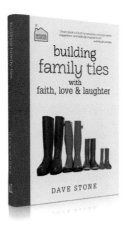

Please share how *Raising Your Kids to Love the Lord* has impacted your family:

WEBSITE: PastorDaveStone.com
FACEBOOK: Facebook.com/FaithfulFamilies
TWITTER: @TheFaithfulFam
TWITTER: @DaveStone920